Opposites
Attract

Written & Illustrated by B. K. Hixson

Copyright 2002 • B. K. Hixson

Opposites Attract

Copyright © 2002
First Printing • April 2002
B. K. Hixson

Published by Loose in the Lab, Inc.
9462 South 560 West
Sandy, Utah 84070

www.looseinthelab.com

Library of Congress Cataloging-in-Publication Data:

Hixson, B. K.
      Opposites Attract/B. K. Hixson, Ed Goffard
      p.   cm.-(Loose in the Lab Science Series)

      Includes glossary and index
      ISBN 0-9660965-1-7
   1. Magnets and magnetism-experiments-juvenile
literature. [1. Magnets-Experiments 2. Experiments]
I.Ed Goffard II. B. K. Hixson III. Loose in the Lab IV.
Title V. Series
QC757.V43   2002
538.4

Printed in the United States of America
Give us a call if you get stuck.

Dedication

Ed Goffard

(Shaver Elementary School • Circa 1967)

Mr. Goffard, who as of this writing, is an alive-and-very-engaged 75 years old, living in the semi-urban wilds of Oregon. But back in 1967 he was my fifth-grade teacher. And at that time neither he nor I knew it, but he spent the year distinguishing himself as the teacher who truly introduced me to science and did so in the context of what scientists do best—pursue the truth through relentless mangling of an experiment until you torture it into revealing the answer that you wish to know.

We spent the year growing huge alum crystals and building dodecahedrons that dangled precariously from the lights. We strung an entire telephone system across the room and, most famously, built electric motors from scratch. It was the motors that we enjoyed the most.

As for you, Mr. G., thanks so much for an exceptional education!

Acknowledgments

There are always a lot of thank-yous that need to be passed out when a book gets published, and this one is no exception. On top of the list is Ed Goffard, my fifth-grade teacher and the person to whom the book is dedicated. As far as I can remember, my first real look at electricity and magnetism came under his supervision. Thanks again!

As for my educational outlook (the hands-on perspective and the use of humor in the classroom), Dr. Fox, my senior professor at Oregon State University, gets the credit for shaping my educational philosophy recognizing that even at the collegiate level we were onto something a little different. He did his very best to encourage, nurture, and support me while I was getting basket loads of opposition for being willing to swim upstream. Also several colleagues did their very best to channel my enthusiasm during those early, formative years of teaching: Dick Bishop, Dick Hinton, Dee Strange, and Linda Zimmermann. Thanks for your patience and support.

I would be remiss if I did not thank the folks at Oregon State University, Dr. Margaret Niess, Dr. Larry Enoch, Maya Ables, and the rest of the Department of Science and Math Education gang for their enthusiasm and support for these kinds of projects and the doors that they open. And thanks to Mr. DeWitt for your overview and valuable critique.

Next up are all the folks that get to do the dirty work that make the final publication look so polished but very rarely get the credit they deserve. Next, our resident graphics gurus, Kris Barton and Sarah Williams each get a nod for scanning and cleaning the artwork that you find on these pages as well as putting together the graphics that make up the cover. All of that is done so that Kathleen Hixson and Diane Burns can take turns simultaneously proofreading the text while mocking my writing skills. Only then is the manuscript handed over to Susan Moore who peruses it with her scanning electon microscope eyes and adds hyphens, commas, capitals, and other formal genera of the grammatical world that have eluded me for decades.

Once the finished product is done, the book has to be printed by the good folks at Excel Graphics—Kurt Warner and the crew, so that Louisa Walker, TracySt.Pierre, Kent Walker, and the Delta Education gang can market, ship the books, collect the money, and send us a couple of nickels. A short thank-you, for a couple of very important jobs.

Mom and Dad, as always, get the end credits. Thanks for the education, encouragement, and love. And for Kathy and the kids—Porter, Shelby, Courtney, and Aubrey—hugs and kisses.

Repro Rights

There is very little about this book that is truly formal, but at the insistence of our wise and esteemed counsel, let us declare: *No part of this book may be reproduced or utilized in any form or by any means, electronic or mechanical, including photocopying, recording, or by any information storage and retrieval system, without permission in writing from the publisher.* That would be us.

More Legal Stuff

Official disclaimer for you aspiring scientists and lab groupies. This is a hands-on science book. By the very intent of the design, you will be directed to use common, nontoxic, household items in a safe and responsible manner to avoid injury to yourself and others who are present while you are pursuing your quest for knowledge and enlightenment in the world of physics. Praise the Almighty and pass the iron filings

If, for some reason, perhaps even beyond your own control, you have an affinity for disaster, we wish you well. *But we, in no way take any responsibility for any injury that is incurred to any person using the information provided in this book or for any damage to personal property or effects that are directly or indirectly a result of the suggested activities contained herein.* Translation: You're on your own. Don't stick your fingers between two magnets that you can't pry apart.

Less Formal Legal Stuff

If you are in need of further clarification or simply choose to ignore this pleasant and polite caution, we will send Kim Chee, our garlic-snarfing personal trainer, to your address. She, in turn, will exhale in your general direction a repeated number of times until you succumb to the haze of fermented cabbage and partially decomposed oriental vegetables. If that does not work, then we will turn our legal counsel loose on you. Guaranteed not to be a pretty sight for onlookers, unless you enjoy those nature movies that feature carnivorous attacks on diseased range animals.

Table of Contents

The National Content Standards (Grades K–4)
C. Heat, Light, Electricity, & Magnetism
• *Magnets attract and repel each other and certain kinds of other materials.*

The 10 Big Ideas About Magnetism & Corresponding Labs

1. Magnets come in different shapes, sizes, and strengths. Lodestone is a naturally occurring magnet.

2. Magnets can be created by touching or rubbing an iron object to a magnet. Heating or hitting that object will destroy its magnetic ability.

3. A magnet can attract some objects but not others. This is a characteristic that can be used to identify different kinds of materials.

4. Magnets are surrounded by an invisible magnetic field that can pass through permeable materials. Materials that do not allow the magnetic field to pass through are called nonpermeable.

5. A compass is a tool used to detect magnetic fields. Magnetic fields can also be detected using iron filings.

6. The Earth is a giant magnet with a North Pole and a South Pole. A magnetic field surrounds the Earth.

Table of Contents

7. Some molecules have both positive and negative ends like the poles of a magnet and are called bipolar or diamagnetic. This characteristic allows these tiny, building blocks to behave like magnets. Water is an excellent example.

8. Magnets have a north pole and a south pole; like poles repel and opposite poles attract. Magnetic fields are stongest at the poles.

9. Magnets can also be created using electricity, and when electricity flows through a wire, it produces a detectable magnetic field.

10. Magnets can be used for technology, medicine, transportation, research, and entertainment.

Science Fair Projects
A Step-by-Step Guide: From Idea to Presentation

Who Are You? And . . .

First of all, we may have an emergency at hand and we'll both want to cut to the chase and get the patient into the cardiac unit if necessary. So, before we go too much further, **define yourself**. Please check one and only one choice listed below and then immediately follow the directions that follow *in italics*. Thank you in advance for your cooperation.

I am holding this book because. . .

   A. I am a responsible, but panicked, parent. My son/daughter/triplets (circle one) just informed me that his/her/their science fair project is due tomorrow. This is the only therapy I could afford on such short notice. Which means that if I was not holding this book, my hands would be encircling the soon-to-be-worm-bait's neck.

Directions: Can't say this is the first or the last time we heard that one. Hang in there, we can do this.

1. Quickly read the Table of Contents with the worm bait. The Big Ideas define what each section is about. Obviously, the kid is not passionate about science, or you would not be in this situation. See if you can find an idea that causes some portion of an eyelid or facial muscle to twitch.

If that does not work, we recommend narrowing the list to the following labs because they are fast, use materials that can be acquired with limited notice, and the intrinsic level of interest is generally quite high.

How to Use This Book

2. *Take the materials list from the lab write-up from page 207 of the Surviving a Science Fair Project section and go shopping.*

3. *Assemble the materials and perform the lab at least once. Gather as much data as you can.*

4. *Go to page 184 and read the material. Then start on Step 1 of Preparing Your Science Fair Project. With any luck you can dodge an academic disaster.*

___ B. I am worm bait. My science fair project is due tomorrow, and there is not anything moldy in the fridge. I need a big Band-Aid, in a hurry.

Directions: Same as Option A. You can decide if and when you want to clue your folks in on your current dilemma.

___ C. I am the parent of a student who informed me that he/ she has been assigned a science fair project due in six to eight weeks. My son/daughter has expressed an interest in science books with humorous illustrations that attempt to explain magnetism and associated phenomena.

Who Are You? And . . .

Directions: Well, you came to the right place. Give your kid these directions and stand back.

1. The first step is to read through the Table of Contents and see if anything grabs your interest. Read through several experiments, see if the science teacher has any of the more difficult materials to acquire like magnets, bell wire, Ferrofluid, and some of the other materials, and ask if they can be borrowed. Play with the experiments and see which one really tickles your fancy.

2. After you have found and conducted an experiment that you like, take a peek at the Science Fair Ideas and see if you would like to investigate one of those or create an idea of your own. The guidelines for those are listed on page 193 in the Surviving Your Science Fair section. You have plenty of time so you can fiddle and fool with the original experiment and its derivations several times. Work until you have an original question you want to answer and then start the process, listed on page 198. You are well on your way to an excellent grade.

___ D. I am a responsible student and have been assigned a science fair project due in six to eight weeks. I am interested in magnetism, and despite demonstrating maturity and wisdom well beyond the scope of my peers, I too still have a sense of humor. Enlighten and entertain me.

Directions: Cool. Being teachers, we have heard reports of this kind of thing happening but usually in an obscure and hard-to-locate town several states removed. Nonetheless, congratulations.

Same as Option C. You have plenty of time and should be able to score very well. We'll keep our eyes peeled when the Nobel Prizes are announced in a couple of years.

How to Use This Book

___ **E. I am a parent who home schools my child/children.** We are always on the lookout for quality curriculum materials that are not only educationally sound but also kid- and teacher-friendly. I am not particularly strong in science, but I realize it is a very important topic. How is this book going to help me out?

Directions: In a lot of ways we created this book specifically for home schoolers.

1. We have taken the National Content Standards, the guidelines that are used by all public and private schools nationwide to establish their curriculum base, and listed them in the Table of Contents. You now know where you stand with respect to the national standards.

2. We then break these standards down and list the major ideas that you should want your kid to know. We call these the Big Ideas. Some people call them objectives, others call them curriculum standards, educational benchmarks, or assessment norms. Same apple, different name. The bottom line is that when your child is done studying this unit on magnets you want them not only to understand and explain each of the 10 Big Ideas listed in this book, but also, to be able to defend and argue their position based on experiential evidence that they have collected.

3. Building on the Big Ideas, we have collected and rewritten 50 hands-on science labs. Each one has been specifically selected so that it supports the Big Idea with which it is correlated. This is critical. As the kids do the science experiment, they see, smell, touch, and hear the experiment. They will store that information in several places in their brains. When it comes time to comprehend the Big Idea, the concrete hands-on experiences provide the foundation for building the Idea, which is quite often abstract. Kids who merely read about magnets, magnetic fields, induced currents and Eddy currents, or who develop an understanding of three-dimensional magnetic fields surrounding the Earth, are trying to build abstract ideas on abstract ideas and quite often miss the mark.

Who Are You? And . . .

For example: I can show you a recipe in a book for chocolate chip cookies and ask you to reiterate it. Or I can turn you loose in a kitchen, have you mix the ingredients, grease the pan, plop the dough on the cookie sheet, slide everything into the oven, and wait impatiently until they pop out eight minutes later. Chances are that the description given by the person who actually made the cookies is going to be much clearer because it is based on their true understanding of the process, **because it is based on experience.**

4. Once you have completed the experiment, there are a number of extension ideas under the Science Fair Extensions that allow you to spend as much or as little time on the ideas as you deem necessary.

5. A word about humor. Science is not usually known for being funny even though Bill Nye, The Science Guy, Beaker from Sesame Street, and Beakman's World do their best to mingle the two. That's all fine and dandy, but we want you to know that we incorporate humor because it is scientifically (and educationally) sound to do so. Plus it's really at the root of our personalities. Here's what we know:

When we laugh . . .
a. Our pupils dilate, increasing the amount of light entering the eye.
b. Our heart rate increases, which pumps more blood to the brain.
c. Oxygen-rich blood to the brain means the brain is able to collect, process, and store more information. Big I.E.: increased comprehension.
d. Laughter relaxes muscles, which can be involuntarily tense if a student is uncomfortable or fearful of an academic topic.
e. Laughter stimulates the immune system, which will ultimately translate into overall health and fewer kids who say they are sick of science.
f. Socially, it provides an acceptable pause in the academic routine, which then gives the student time to regroup and prepare to address some of the more difficult ideas with a renewed spirit. They can study longer and focus on ideas more efficiently.
g. Laughter releases chemicals in the brain that are associated with pleasure and joy.
6. If you follow the book in the order it is written, you will be able to build ideas and concepts in a logical and sequential pattern. But that is by no means necessary. For a complete set of guidelines on our ideas on how to teach home-schooled kids science, check out our book, Why's the Cat on Fire? How to Excel at Teaching Science to Your Home-Schooled Kids.

How to Use This Book

___ F. **I am a public/private school teacher,** and this looks like an interesting book to add ideas to my classroom lesson plans.

Directions: It is, and please feel free to do so. However, while this is a great classroom resource for kids, may we also recommend two other titles Fi Ling's Portable Motor Design Shop *if you wish to teach magnetism to fourth through sixth graders and* Magnet Mania *for the K–3 range.*

These two books have teacher-preparation pages, student-response sheets or lab pages, lesson plans, bulletin board ideas, discovery center ideas, vocabulary sheets, unit pretests, unit exams, lab practical exams, and student grading sheets. Basically everything you need if you are a science nincompoop, and a couple of cool ideas if you are a seasoned veteran with an established curriculum. All of the ideas that are covered in this one book are covered much more thoroughly in the other two. They were specifically written for teachers.

___ G. **My son/daughter/grandson/niece/father-in-law** is interested in science, and this looks like fun.

Directions: Congratulations on your selection. Add a gift certificate to the local science supply store and a package of hot chocolate mix and you have the perfect rainy Saturday afternoon gig.

___ H. **Every time I walk by my refrigerator I find that my new cobalt-neodium hip is attracted to the the front panel and it takes me five minutes to pry myself loose and that is if I don't get myself hung up on the ice maker. Oy vey! Can you help?**

Directions: Nope. Try seeing your Rabbi.

Lab Safety

Contained herein are 50 science activities to help you better understand the nature and characteristics of magnets as we currently understand these things. However, since you are on your own in this journey we thought it prudent to share some basic wisdom and experience in the safety department.

Read the Instructions

An interesting concept, especially if you are a teenager. Take a minute before you jump in and get going to read all of the instructions as well as warnings. If you do not understand something, stop and ask an adult for help.

Clean Up All Messes

Keep your lab area clean. It will make it easier to put everything away at the end and may also prevent contamination and the subsequent germination of a species of mutant tomato bug larva. You will also find that chemicals perform with more predictability if they are not poisoned with foreign molecules.

Organize

Translation: Put it back where you get it. If you need any more clarification, there is an opening at the landfill for you.

Dispose of Poisons Properly

This will not be much of a problem with labs that use, study, and measure magnets. However, if you happen to wander over into one of the many disciplines that incorporates the use of chemicals, then we would suggest that you use great caution with the materials and definitely dispose of any and all poisons properly.

Practice Good Fire Safety

If there is a fire in the room, notify an adult immediately. If an adult is not in the room and the fire is manageable, smother the outbreak with a fire blanket or use a fire extinguisher. When the fire is contained, immediately send someone to find an adult. If, for any reason, you happen to catch on fire, **REMEMBER: Stop, Drop, and Roll.** Never run; it adds oxygen to the fire, making it burn faster, and it also scares the bat guano out of the neighbors when they see the neighbor kids running down the block doing an imitation of a campfire marshmallow without the stick.

Protect Your Skin

It is a good idea to always wear protective gloves whenever you are working with chemicals. Again, this particular book does not suggest or incorporate chemicals in its lab activities very often. However, when we do, we are incorporating only safe, manageable kinds of chemicals for these labs. If you do happen to spill a chemical on your skin, notify an adult immediately and then flush the area with water for 15 minutes. It's unlikely, but if irritation develops, have your parents or another responsible adult look at it. If it appears to be of concern, contact a physician. Take any information that you have about the chemical with you.

Lab Safety

Save Your Nose Hairs

Sounds like a cause celebre LA style, but it is really good advice. To smell a chemical to identify it, hold the open container six to ten inches down and away from your nose. Make a clockwise circular motion with your hand over the opening of the container, "wafting" some of the fumes toward your nose. This will allow you to safely smell some of the fumes without exposing youself to a large dose of anything noxious. This technique may help prevent a nosebleed or your lungs from accidentally getting burned by chemicals.

Wear Goggles If Appropriate

If the lab asks you to heat or mix chemicals, be sure to wear protective eyewear. Also have an eyewash station or running water available. You never know when something is going to splatter, splash, or react unexpectedly. It is better to look like a nerd and be prepared than schedule a trip down to pick out a Seeing Eye dog. If you do happen to accidentally get chemicals in your eye, flush the area for 15 minutes. If any irritation or pain develops, immediately go see a doctor.

Lose the Comedy Routine

You should have plenty of time scheduled during your day to mess around, but science lab is not one of them. Horseplay breaks glassware, spills chemicals, and creates unnecessary messes—things that parents do not appreciate. Trust us on this one.

No Eating

Do not eat while performing a lab. Putting your food in the lab area contaminates your food and the experiment. This makes for bad science and worse indigestion. Avoid poisoning yourself and goobering up your lab ware by observing this rule.

Happy and safe experimenting!

Recommended Materials Suppliers

For every lesson in this book we offer a list of materials. Many of these are very easy to acquire, and if you do not have them in your home already, you will be able to find them at the local grocery or hardware store. For more difficult items we have selected, for your convenience, a small but respectable list of suppliers who will meet your needs in a timely and economical manner. Call for a catalog or quote on the item that you are looking for, and they will be happy to give you a hand.

Loose in the Lab
9462 South 560 West
Sandy, Utah 84070
Phone 1-888-403-1189
Fax 1-801-568-9586
www.looseinthelab.com

Delta Education
80 NW Boulevard
Nashua, NH 03063
Phone 1-800-442-5444
Fax 1-800-282-9560
www.delta-ed.com

Nasco
901 Jonesville Ave.
Fort Atkinson, Wisconsin 53538
Phone 1-414-563-2446
Fax 1-920-563-8296
www.nascofa.com

Ward's Scientific
5100 W Henrietta Road
Rochester, New York 14692
Phone 800-387-7822
Fax 1-716-334-6174
www.wardsci.com

Educational Innovations
151 River Road
Cos Cob, Conneticut 06807
Phone 1-888-912-7474
Fax 1-203-629-2739
www.teachersource.com

The Magnet Source
PO Box 279
Castle Rock, Colorado 80104
Phone 800-525-3536
www.magnet cource.com

Edmund Scientific
101 E. Gloucester Pike
Barrington, NJ 08007
Phone 1-(800) 728-6999
Fax 1-856-547-3292
www.edmundscientific.com

Sargent Welch Scientific Co.
911 Commerce Court
Buffalo Grove, Illinois 60089
Phone 800-727-4368
Fax 1-800-676-2540
www.sargentwelch.com

The Ideas, Lab Activities, & Science Fair Extensions

Big Idea 1

Magnets come in different shapes, sizes, and strengths. Lodestone is a naturally occurring magnet.

Magnet Montage

The Experiment

Welcome to the study of magnets and magnetism. Wishing to leave no stone unturned and no idea without a presentation, we are going to start at the very beginning and introduce you to the different shapes that magnets can take.

This will serve two purposes. One, we will know that we have truly started at the beginning of this unit, and two, there will be no confusion about which kind of magnet we are recommending that you use for a particular activity.

Materials

1   Donut magnet
1   Bar magnet
1   Book magnet
1   Cow magnet
1   Horseshoe magnet
1   Piece of lodestone

Procedure

1. Match the shapes of the magnets with their proper names by drawing a line to connect them. Check your answers on page 24.

2. On page 24 is a picture of a frog that is drawn using the shapes of the different kinds of magnets. Your task is to color the pictures there using the colors matched to the different magnet shapes. For example, when you see the shape of a horseshoe magnet you would color it green. Use the following key to color your pictures.

book: blue   donut: orange
horseshoe: green   bar: red
cow: yellow

Data & Observations

1. Donut   A.

2. Horseshoe   B.

3. Book   C.

4. Cow   D.

5. Bar   E.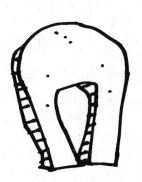

Magnet Montage

Data & Observations

How Come, Huh?

Because we said so, that's why. OK, we'll be serious for a bit. This idea is about as fundamental as they come. Magnets have different shapes. If that explanation needs explaining, we are at a loss to help. Answers to match: 1-D, 2-E, 3-A, 4-B, and 5-C.

Science Fair Extensions

1. Construct a picture of anything you would like on a separate piece of paper using the shapes of the different kinds of magnets: ring, circular, horseshoe, bar, and cow.

2. Go on a magnet scavenger hunt and find other shapes and kinds of magnets. In particular, magnets that are made and marketed to attach to the outside of refrigerators come in any number of interesting shapes and sizes. There are also magnetized pieces of metal that are sold with a base that allow you to mold and change the shapes that they take.

Magnet Tug o' War

The Experiment

A contest! Which magnet is the strongest? We are going to use three different magnets and measure how far away they can get before they attract each of those items. The implication, of course, is that the strongest magnet will attract the objects from the greatest distance— an old Star Trek concept, we suspect.

Materials

1   Metric ruler
1   Iron ball bearing (bb)
1   Cow magnet
1   Donut magnet
1   Bar magnet
1   Book magnet
1   Horseshoe magnet
1   Piece of lodestone
1   Small paper clip
1   Straight pin

Procedure

1. Place the metric ruler on a hard, smooth, flat surface. Start with the iron ball bearing (bb) by placing it at the zero centimeter (0 cm) mark at the end of the ruler. Place the cow magnet at the other end of the ruler near the thirty centimeter (30 cm) mark.

2. When you are ready to go, slowly slide the cow magnet toward the bb. At some point the bb is going to be attracted to the cow magnet and roll across and "stick" to it. Record the distance the cow magnet is from the bb in the data table on the next page.

Magnet Tug o' War

3. Repeat this procedure using the bb and attracting it with the four other kinds of magnets. Repeat the experiment testing the pin and small paper clip. Record the distances that you observe in the data table below.

Data & Observations

Record the distance that the magnet was from each item when you tested it. When you have collected the data, plot in the graph on the next page using the key at the bottom of this page.

Magnet Type	Object Being Attracted		
	Ball Bearing	Paper Clip	Straight Pin
Cow			
Donut			
Horseshoe			
Book			
Bar			
Lodestone			

When you construct your graph use the following key to identify the different items that are being attracted to the magnets.

ball bearings: dots   • • • • •

paper clips: dashed lines   ▬ ▬ ▬

straight pins: solid line   ▬▬▬▬▬

20					
18					
16					
14					
12					
10					
8					
6					
4					
2					
0					

Cow   Donut   Horseshoe   Book   Bar   Lodestone

How Come, Huh?

The strength of a magnet depends on several factors, the least of which is temperature so we are going to throw that one out. The other three are more important. The purer the iron sample, the stronger the magnet; the more iron atoms, the stronger the magnet; and the better organized the iron atoms in the sample are, the stronger the magnet will be. In this case the cow magnet is the largest, heaviest, and best organized of the three magnets so it attracts iron objects from the greatest distance.

Science Fair Extensions

3. Design an experiment that allows you to change the uphill angle that the objects travel to get to the magnet and plot how that angle affects the distance the magnet attracts the objects.

A Magnet, Naturally

The Experiment

You are going to experiment with a magnetic mineral called lodestone and explore its properties. Lodestone is a variety of the iron-rich mineral magnetite, but it is unique in that it is naturally magnetic. In fact, it acts just like a regular bar magnet, influencing the position of a compass needle, lining up with the natural magnetic poles of the Earth if it is suspended, and quickly acquiring a fuzzy, metallic beard if it is accidentally dropped in a pile of iron filings.

We've given you a pretty good outline as far as this lab goes, so we'll just turn you loose.

Materials

1   Piece of string, 12 inches long
1   Sample of lodestone
1   Bar magnet
1   Plastic baggie
1   Shaker of iron filings
1   Sheet of paper
1   Packet of salt
1   Compass

Procedure

1. Tie one end of the string around the middle of the lodestone and hold it so that it can rotate freely. Bring the north end of the bar magnet near the lodestone and observe how the mineral responds to the magnetic field of the magnet. What you have created is a very simple compass.

Remove the magnet and the lodestone rotates back to a certain position. It is aligned with the Earth's magnetic field.

2. Place the lodestone in the plastic baggie. Pour a small sample of iron filings out onto the piece of paper and dip the lodestone in them. Observe what happens to the filings when they come in contact with the mineral. You now have a bearded baggie. Remove the lodestone from the baggie over the pile of filings and observe what happens to the filings that were stuck to the baggie.

3. Lodestone can be used to separate substances. Open a salt packet. Pour the salt packet on the iron filings and mix them together thoroughly with your fingers. Run the sample of lodestone (keep it in the baggie) around in the mixture of iron and salt on the paper. You will observe that the iron filings are attracted to the magnet, but the salt crystals are not. When you are done, return the filings to the container and toss the salt in the garbage.

4. Finally, in the space provided on the next page trace the outline of your piece of lodestone in the center of the circles, over the X. When you have traced the outline of the lodestone, leave it in place. Then place your compass in the first circle and observe where the needle points. Remove the compass and draw a replica of the needle position. Do that for all six circles.

When you are done, discuss what you see with an adult. We will get into magnetic fields in later labs—this is just an introduction.

A Magnet, Naturally

Data & Observations

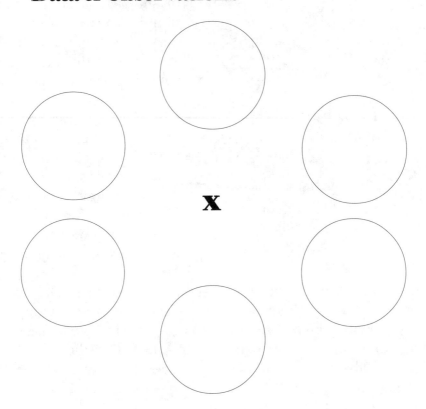

How Come, Huh?

Lodestone contains iron particles that have been naturally lined up. All of the effects that you have been observing are the by-product of the magnetic field that is created by these particles.

Science Fair Extensions

4. Make a list of 25 different objects that you can mix with iron filings and still separate with lodestone.

5. Design and build a compass using lodestone as the needle.

6. Determine if the shape of the lodestone affects the pattern of its magnetic field.

Big Idea 2

Magnets can be created by touching or rubbing an iron object to a magnet. Heating or hitting that object will destroy its magnetic ability.

Chain Reaction

The Experiment

We know that magnets exist. In fact, you probably have a fistful of them staring at you from the front of your refrigerator. So, this first lab is designed to introduce you to the idea that the characteristics of a magnet can be induced, or passed, when certain materials simply come in contact with a magnetic field. In other words, that magnetism can be "passed" from one object to another and then to another with only the first object actually touching the magnet.

Your specific task for this lab is to take several different materials, and first of all, test them to see if they are attracted to the magnet. Then once you identify the materials that are attracted, you will test each item to see if you can hang a chain of those items from the magnet—proving the idea that the magnetic field in the magnet can be passed from one item to another.

Materials

1	Sheet of paper
1	Pair of scissors
1	Cow magnet
15	Small paper clips
15	Straight pins
15	Iron ball bearings (bb's)
15	Brass brads
5	Poker chips
3	Craft sticks

Procedure

1. The first thing that you are going to want to do is fill in the second column, Material, of the data table on page 34, by identifying what each material is made from. Your choices are metal, plastic, paper, or wood.

2. Cut several small pieces of paper from the sheet of paper. Each piece should be about half an inch wide and an inch long. You don't have to be exact. When the paper has been prepared, test each item in your data table with the magnet. Determine which ones are attracted to the magnet and which ones are not. Record your observations in the third column of the data table, Magnetic (Y/N), by writing a *Y* if it sticks to the magnet and a *N* if it does not.

3. You should have discovered in your testing that iron bb's are attracted to the magnet. Add an iron bb to the rounded end of the cow magnet. Then add a second iron bb to the first, then a third to the second, and so on. Use the illustration to the right as a guide.

4. Hang one bb off the end of the previous one. When you can no longer add any bb's to the chain, record the *maximum* number of iron bb's that are hanging off the cow magnet. This number can be entered next to bb's in the fourth column named, # Items Hung.

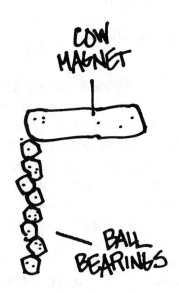

5. Repeat this procedure with the other objects that were attracted to the magnet. Record the *maximum* number of each item you test in the data table.

Chain Reaction

Data & Observations

Record the *maximum* number of straight pins, paper clips, paper strips, brads, craft sticks, poker chips, and bb's that you got to hang off of the cow magnet in the data table below.

Item Tested	Material	Magnetic (Y/N)	# Items Hung
Straight Pins			
Poker Chips			
Paper Clips			
Brads			
Craft Sticks			
Ball Bearings (bb's)			
Paper Strips			

How Come, Huh?

The iron particles in the magnet are organized and lined up in an orderly fashion. When this happens, a magnetic field is produced that attracts other iron objects. When these other iron objects come close to the magnet, they also line up in the magnetic field of the magnet, and this produces another, weaker magnetic field. At some point the weight of the object is greater than the strength of the magnetic field that is attracting it, and it falls off the chain. The brads don't work at all because they are made of copper and steel and do not have enough iron to be attracted to the magnet. Paper is not magnetic and neither is plastic or wood, but we'll let you prove that to yourself in another lab.

Science Fair Extensions

7. Re-create the experiment and use the same materials, but substitute different kinds of magnets. Create a data table that allows you to record the strengths of the different magnets that you test and then graph that data for easy comparison.

8. Design an experiment that explores how the shape of a material affects its ability to form chains. For example, bb's, straight pins, and paper clips are made of iron that has been formed into different shapes. Find three other iron objects that also have different shapes and determine if the shape of an object affects its ability to form chains.

9. Do this experiment with a friend so she understands the idea you are exploring and then write sequences of different objects on a piece of paper and ask her to predict if and where the chain will fall apart. For example, Chain 1: paper clip, paper clip, bb, brad, pin, bb, and pin. Chain 2: bb, bb, pin, paper clip, bb, pin, and brad. Chain 3: brad, brad, bb, pin, paper clip, and pin. Take turns inventing chains and testing each other.

10. Make a chain of bb's hanging off the end of a magnet. Gently remove the chain from the magnet by grabbing the top bb. Hold the chain of bb's over the palm of your hand and watch as the bb's fall off one by one. Why did they fall off?

Magnet Thief

The Experiment

Some magnets are very strong, and when they get their magnetic fields around an iron object, it becomes very difficult to pry the object loose—unless you use a nail.

This lab will show you how you can induce, or create, a magnetic field in a nail that becomes stronger than the magnet that it is touching. When this happens, you will be able to use the nail to swipe a bb from the bigger, stronger magnet.

Materials

1   Nail, 6-penny, ungalvanized
1   Iron ball bearing (bb)
1   Magnet

Procedure

1.   Test your nail and make sure that it is not already magnetized. To do this, hold it close to the bb. If it is not magnetized, it will not attract the bb. This is good.

(If your nail is attracted to the bb, simply find a hard, concrete surface and toss the nail on the ground several times. This will discombobulate, or mess up, the atoms in the nail and neutralize the magnetic field that you have going.)

2.   Pick up the bb with the magnet. Bring the point of the nail to the bb and touch it. Use the illustration to the upper right as a guide. With the very point of the nail touching the bb, count to five.

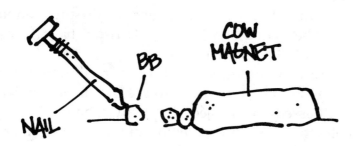

3. Pull the nail away from the magnet and the bb will stick to the nail.

How Come, Huh?

When you touched the bb to the magnet, the magnetic field passed into the bb. It stands to reason then that when you touched the nail to the bb, the magnetic field continued on down the line—as we found in the previous experiment—and it now influences the nail also.

Why did the "skinny" nail steal the bb from the "fat" magnet? Usually the big guy is stronger, right? Not in this case—when they are in contact, the magnetic field is shared equally between the magnet and the nail. Because the nail is skinny, the field is more concentrated and is therefore able to steal the bb from the bigger magnet.

Science Fair Extensions

11. Add bb's to the magnet and determine what happens when there are two, three, four, and five bb's between the magnet and the nail. Do you get the same reaction each time or a different reaction? Why?

12. Try nails of different sizes. Is there a point at which the nail becomes so large that the magnetic field is less concentrated than the magnetic field of the magnet and the bb cannot be stolen? Can a nail be too small?

Impromptu Magnets

The Experiment

Congratulations! You have successfully proven that a magnetic field can be passed from iron object to iron object if those objects are in *direct contact* with the magnet.

We are very impressed with your intellect and persistence. The challenge before you now is to see if a magnetic field can be induced, or passed, to an object simply by rubbing that object with the magnet—theoretically organizing, or lining up, the iron atoms so that they have their own magnetic field.

Materials

1	16-Penny nail, ungalvanized
1	Large paper clip
1	Plastic straw
1	Wooden craft stick
1	Plastic poker chip
1	Brass brad
1	Plastic pipette, 1 mL
1	Cow magnet
1	Rectangular magnet
1	Finger (yours)
1	Pile of straight pins (15 or so)

Procedure

1. The first thing that you are going to want to do is fill in the second column, Material, of the data table on page 40, by identifying what each object is made from. Your choices are metal, plastic, paper, flesh, or wood.

2. You are going to test ten different items for the presence of a magnetic field by dipping them in a pile of straight pins. If a magnetic field is present, that object will pick up a couple of straight pins.

3. Mark a Y in the third column, Magnetic Field, of the data table on the next page for every item that has a magnetic field. Eliminate those objects before doing the second test described in instructions 4–5.

4. One at a time, each of the items that remain is then stroked 50 times, one way, with a strong magnet.

After it has been stroked 50 times, it is dipped in the pile of pins and tested again to see if a magnetic field has been induced.

5. Mark a Y in the fourth column of the data table on the next page if a magnetic field has been induced, or passed, and also record the number of pins that the object picked up.

For best results lower each of the objects parallel to the table, exposing the largest possible surface area. The top illustration on the right will give you a good idea.

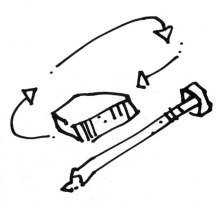

Impromptu Magnets

Data & Observations

Record the type of material that each item is made from. Then test each item for a magnetic field and mark a *Y* for yes or *N* for no. Finally, test the items without magnetic fields for an induced magnetic field and mark a *Y* or *N* in the last column labeled, Induced Field, along with a slash and the number of pins (/#) that were picked up.

Item Tested	Material	Magnetic Field	Induced Field
Nail			
Paper clip			
Straw			
Craft stick			
Poker chip			
Brad			
Pipette, 1 mL			
Cow magnet			
Donut magnet			
Finger (yours)			

How Come, Huh?

The nail and paper clip are both made up trillions of *iron* atoms. Most of the time these atoms are disorganized and sitting in a very random pattern, pointing different directions. Imagine a box full of straight pins—they are pointing every which way and there appears to be no organization at all—and you are starting to get the picture. Now imagine that those straight pins are floating in water and can rotate in any direction they want and you are getting a better idea.

As you bring the magnet near the nail and start to stroke it over the surface, the magnetic field of the magnet starts tugging and organizing the iron atoms in the nail. After several strokes, many of the iron atoms are lined up in the same direction—this lining up in the same direction is what creates the magnetic field in the atom. The illustration to the right shows what happens when the atoms are lined up and working together.

If an object does not contain iron, then the magnetic field of the magnet has very little influence on that object. That is why the wood, plastic, and your finger did not attract any pins, but they are good to test anyway so that you have something to compare the iron objects with—for reference.

Extensions

13. Expand the test group to include other items. You can either test more of the same kind of material or add new items like glass, cloth, paper, Styrofoam, and other kinds of metals in addition to iron. Create an expanded version of the data table and repeat the experiment.

14. Design an experiment that examines the relationship between the size of the nail and the strength of the magnetic field that is created. Is bigger better? That would be the question of the day.

deMagnetizing Nails

The Experiment

Assuming you are going through the book in order, you now know that magnets can pass their magnetic fields to other iron objects. You also have found that magnetic fields can be induced, or created, in iron objects. The next question is what can you do to reverse the process?

This lab will allow you to explore what happens when nails that have been magnetized are demagnetized by throwing them on the ground, as well as by pounding them with a hammer.

Materials

1   16-Penny nail, ungalvanized
1   Magnet
1   Compass
1   Hammer

Procedure

1. Magnetize the nail just like you did in the previous lab by stroking it 50 times, one way, with a strong magnet. After it has been stroked 50 times, bring it close to a compass. If the needle deflects toward the nail, you have accomplished your first task.

2. To demagnetize an object all you have to do is scramble the iron atoms inside it. This can be done by tossing the nail onto a hard surface, like concrete or asphalt, a couple of times.

After you have tossed the nail, pick it up and bring it near the compass again and observe what happens this time.

3. Remagnetize the nail with the magnet. Check it with the compass and then take a hammer and whap the nail 10 times. Test the nail using the compass and see if the magnetism was destroyed when you whapped the nail with the hammer.

How Come, Huh?

The nail is made up trillions of *iron* atoms. Most of the time these atoms are pointing in different directions. As you bring the magnet near the nail and start to stroke it over the surface of the nail, the magnetic field of the magnet starts tugging and organizing the iron atoms in the nail. After several strokes, many of the iron atoms are lined up in the same direction. This lining up in the same direction is what creates the magnetic field in the nail. If you did the previous experiment, this should all sound eerily familiar.

When you toss the nail to the ground or whack it with the hammer, you are jarring the atoms inside the nail. This causes them to become disoriented. When the atoms become disoriented, they do not work together to create the magnetic field that you previously observed.

Science Fair Extensions

15. Explore the relationship between the size of the nail and how easy it is to magnetize it as well as demagnetize it. Does size matter when it comes to magnetic fields?

16. You can drop them, you can whack them. How else can you get magnetism to disappear?

Curie Point

The Experiment

You have a pretty good idea by now that magnets are attracted to iron objects. We have also demonstrated that objects that are magnetized can be demagnetizing by throwing them on the ground or whacking them with a hammer. We are going to combine these two ideas to introduce the Curie point to you.

This lab, inspired by the Exploratorium Science Snacks Series, rounds out the experiments for Big Idea 2. A magnet is normally attracted to a piece of iron. If an iron wire gets too hot—called the Curie point, the wire loses its ability to be magnetized.

Materials

1	Box of Tinkertoys
1	Donut magnet
1	12-Inch piece of cotton string
1	12-Inch piece of single-strand, iron wire
2	Alligator clips
1	6-Volt lantern battery
1	Clock with sweep second hand or stopwatch
1	12-Inch piece of double-strand, iron wire
1	12-Inch piece of triple-strand, iron wire

Procedure

1. Using four wheels and six wooden posts from your pile of Tinkertoys, build the setup that is pictured in the upper right-hand portion of the next page. Or, if you choose, a wire hanger wrapped in masking tape and bent into a similar shape will also work nicely.

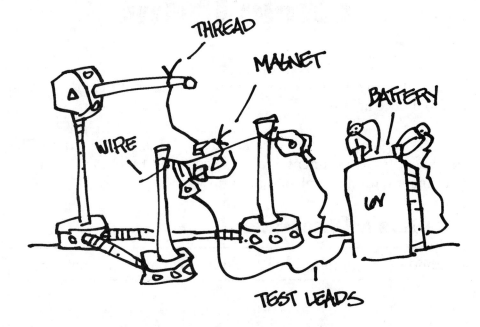

2. Tie one end of the string to the top wood post extending out over the lab and tie the other end of the string to the donut magnet.

3. Wrap the single-strand piece of iron wire between the two posts attached to the center post.

4. Move the magnet so that it comes in contact with the iron wire and sticks to it. If there is a lot of slack in the wire, wrap the other end of the string around the wood post so that it looks like the drawing above.

5. Attach one alligator lead to each post of the battery and the positive lead to the iron wire. Do not connect the other lead until you are ready to time the experiment.

6. Note the beginning time in the Data & Observations section and attach the second alligator lead to the iron wire. As the electricity flows, the wire will heat up. When it heats to the point where it loses its ability to produce a magnetic field—the Curie point, the magnet will release from the wire and swing freely. When this happens, record the time on page 46.

Curie Point

7. Let the wire cool and you will notice that the magnet will stick to it once again.

8. Replace the single-strand wire with the double-strand wire and repeat the experiment again. Record the time and repeat the experiment with the triple-strand wire.

Data & Observations

# Strands	Beginning Time	Ending Time	Actual Time
1			
2			
3			

How Come, Huh?

As the iron particles in the wire get hotter and hotter, they start to wiggle around. The wire expands, everything loosens up. When this happens the atoms lose their ability to line up, work together, and form a magnetic field. The magnet releases from the wire when the temperature gets hot enough and no magnetic field is produced. When the wire cools down, the atoms can once again realign and will attract the magnet.

Science Fair Extensions

17. Experiment with a single strand of wire but change the distance between the leads. Graph your data and explain why the times change.

18. Repeat the experiment but substitute copper wire.

Big Idea 3

A magnet can attract some objects but not others. This is a characteristic that can be used to identify different kinds of materials.

The Magnetic Finger

The Experiment

This is an experiment that is just for fun and to make your friends think. You are going to pretend to "magnetize" the finger of your friend, and use it to attract and move a glass-and-rubber eyedropper. This is not well grounded in actual scientific theory, but it's a great way to get the kids to think.

A clean, empty, 2-liter pop bottle is filled with water. An eyedropper that is partially filled with water is placed inside the bottle where it floats. The bottle is capped; and when you place your hands on the sides of the bottle and squeeze, the pressure on the bottle increases causing the eyedropper to gradually sink to the bottom of the jug; when you release the sides, the eyedropper rises again. The name for this contraption is Cartesian Diver. You, however, are going to use it to create the illusion of a magnetic finger.

Materials

1   Glass eyedropper with bulb
1   2-Liter pop bottle, clean, empty
1   Drinking glass
1   Cow magnet
1   Finger, kid attached
     Water

Procedure

1. Fill the 2-liter pop bottle completely full of water.

2. Squeeze the rubber bulb on the top of the eyedropper and dunk the opening of the glass end into a glass of water. Release the bulb, and as you do this, you will notice that the glass portion of the dropper fills with water.

Remove the dropper from the water and squeeze the bulb gently, forcing water out of the eyedropper so that it is approximately half full. To test your eyedropper for buoyancy simply place it back in the glass of water. If it floats, you are in business. If it sinks, your eyedropper is a little too heavy—all you have to do is gently squeeze out a little more water and test it again.

BULB

WATER LEVEL

EYEDROPPER

3. When you get an eyedropper to float, you are ready to place it in the pop bottle and screw the cap on firmly. It should float at the top of the bottle. Now it is time for some fun . . .

4. Here is the premise, tell your friend the following things:

A. We know that magnets can be rubbed on *iron* objects and induce, or create, a magnetic field. It worked very nicely with paper clips and nails.

B. We know that fingers are full of blood and one of the principal components of blood is *iron*.

C. It follows that if you take a magnet and rub it on your finger, you will magnetize the *iron* in the blood and induce a magnetic field—just like with the nail.

The Magnetic Finger

5. Tell your friend that it is now time to "magnetize" his finger. Ask him to hold his pointer finger straight up and down. Take the cow magnet and rub the finger 10 times.

6. Inform him that his finger is now magnetized, and it will attract the eyedropper in the bottle. Pick the bottle up, both hands on the sides, see the cartoon at the top of the page. Ask your friend to place his index finger on the top of the bottle and gently move it down the side.

As he moves his finger, you gently squeeze the sides of the bottle and the dropper will fall, matching the movement of his finger. When he gets to the bottom, ask him to go back up to the top. Follow his finger by releasing the pressure on the bottle so the dropper will rise. It will take some practice, but you can get to the point where you can mimic your friend's actions perfectly, and your friend will think you have magnetized his finger.

How Come, Huh?

1. How did the eyedropper get magnetized?
It didn't, glass and rubber, by themselves, cannot be magnetized. The Big Guy made that decision a long time ago.

2. How did the finger get magnetized?
Pay attention, it didn't.

3. Why did the eyedropper follow the finger?
This happened because you squeezed the bottle just right. The eyedropper moves as a function of increased pressure inside the bottle. When you squeeze the sides of the bottle with your hands, you are mashing the water molecules inside the bottle together, which, incidentally, they don't particularly care for. They, in turn, look for something else to mash, which happens to be the air molecules inside the eyedropper. The water goes inside the eyedropper and pushes up on the air. This added water makes the eyedropper a little more dense overall. When things become more dense, they don't float as well, and, in fact, may not float at all. This makes the eyedropper sink.

When you release the pressure on the sides of the bottle, the air molecules inside the eyedropper get mad (not really, we are taking literary liberties here) and tell the water molecules to knock it off and get out of the eyedropper, which they do. When the water gets pushed out, the overall density of the eyedropper becomes less and it becomes more buoyant, until you press on the sides of the bottle again. All of this creates the illusion that your friend's finger is magnetic.

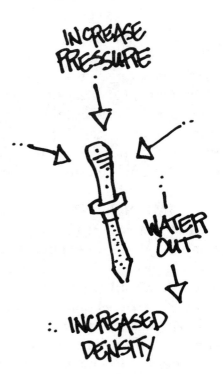

INCREASE PRESSURE

WATER OUT

∴ INCREASED DENSITY

What Is Magnetic?

The Experiment

This lab is an excellent follow-up after you have discussed the answer to getting The Magnetic Finger to work with an adult. In fact, many ancient scholars believed that The Magnetic Finger is challenge enough to build the idea that only iron objects are attracted to magnets. However, we are of a different opinion.

The challenge before you today is to find and test 6 items made of glass, plastic, wood, cloth, metal, and fabric. List the items in the data tables provided, test them to see if they are magnetic, and record your responses to the tests.

Materials

1   Ceramic magnet
30   Assorted objects found around the room

Procedure

1. Collect items from each of the five categories. List those materials in your data tables. Add materials until you have 5 different samples from each of the categories. Test the items that you have recorded in the data table and determine if they are magnetic or not.

IMPORTANT: Keep your magnets away from computers, computer disks, television screens, videotapes, and cassette tapes. These items all work by arranging charged particles in a particular order, which is interpreted by the machines as information. The magnetic field of the magnet may damage that information.

2. After you have collected as much information as you can, discuss and develop a law of magnetism with your friends based on your observations. Determine what is and is not attracted to the magnets according to your observations. Write your finalized law of magnetism in the space provided on page 56. What is and is not attracted to the magnets according to your observations.

Data & Observations

List 6 items all made of the same material in the spaces provided below. Once your list is complete, test each item with a magnet and determine if it has a magnetic field. Mark the response in your data tables.

Item Tested	Material (Glass)	Magnetic (Y/N)
1.		
2.		
3.		
4.		
5.		
6.		

What Is Magnetic?

Item Tested	Material (Plastic)	Magnetic (Y/N)
1.		
2.		
3.		
4.		
5.		
6.		

Item Tested	Material (Wood)	Magnetic (Y/N)
1.		
2.		
3.		
4.		
5.		
6.		

Item Tested	Material (Cloth)	Magnetic (Y/N)
1.		
2.		
3.		
4.		
5.		
6.		

Item Tested	Material (Metal)	Magnetic (Y/N)
1.		
2.		
3.		
4.		
5.		
6.		

What Is Magnetic?

Item Tested	Material (Fabric)	Magnetic (Y/N)
1.		
2.		
3.		
4.		
5.		
6.		

My law of magnetism:_____

_____

_____

How Come, Huh?

Iron, cobalt, nickel, and a few other mixtures of metals (called alloys) create magnetic fields under the right conditions. By the same token, you will figure out very quickly that glass, wood, plastic, cloth, any natural fiber or tissue, and some metals, most notably silver and gold, will not be attracted to the magnet. The metals that are attracted line up in a positive to negative pattern and create a magnetic field.

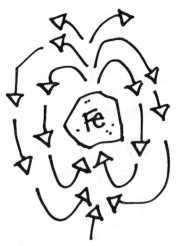

Science Fair Extensions

19. Expand the test group to include other items. You can either test more of the same kind of material or add new items like Styrofoam, organic matter, paper, and other kinds of materials.

20. Another fun zinger is to demonstrate the "magnetic personality" of George Washington. Suspend a crisp new dollar bill so that it is hanging vertically. Bring the ceramic magnet near the bill, which will be attracted to the magnet. The ink that is used to print dollar bills contains particles of iron.

21. Biochemists have used a process called gel electrophoresis for a couple of decades now, which incorporates the use of magnetism to separate long, complex molecules from one another. The way it works is that they "shake" the molecules loose from one another and then expose them to a weak magnetic current. These long molecules that have positive and negative ends then migrate toward one pole or the other. Scientists use this as a way to separate and identify complex molecules, proteins, and other macromolecules. You can recreate a simpler version of this experiment with a little research and help from your local high school chemistry teacher.

22. Our rule of magnetism reads like this: Magnets will attract other magnets and some metal objects. Do a little research and find out who first wrote about magnetism, what they believed caused the phenomena that they were observing, and the experiments that they conducted to explore it.

Fishing with Magnets

The Experiment

Fi Ling is very pleased with your progress. As a reward, you are going to play a fishing game. But, instead of using a hook and bait, you are going to fish using a magnet. Not only that, but we are going to ask you to predict which animals you will be able to catch using your magnet and which you will not be able to catch.

Materials

1   Photocopier
1   Box of crayons
1   Pair of scissors
5   Brass brads
5   Paper clips
1   Large bowl
1   Wooden dowel, 18" to 30"
1   24" Length of cotton string
1   Ring magnet
1   Strip of masking tape

Procedure

1. Prepare the animals. On pages 61 and 62, you will find a number of animals: fish, a shark, a sea urchin, a crab, and a jellyfish. Photocopy, color, and cut them out. Or, if you are feeling creative, draw your own animals. You will need to have 10 animals.

2. Once the animals are copied, colored, and cut out, put brass "eyes" on the animals listed in the left-hand column on page 59. The others are going to have paper clip "eyes." Place all of your fish in the large bowl on the floor.

Brass Eyes	Paper clip Eyes
Jellyfish	Shark
Eel	Flounder
Clam	Salmon
Sea Urchin	Catfish
Crab	Trout

3. Once you have prepared your fish, you are going to want to predict which animals you are going to catch with your magnet and which ones will elude you. Mark your predictions in the data table on the next page.

4. Once your aquatic zoo is complete, you will need to figure out where the pond, lake, or ocean is going to be located. Typically the fish are placed in a bowl and you will fish from your desk.

If you want to make it a little fancier, you could always have a big pan, tub, garbage can, or even make a cardboard pool. Then go fishing. You will notice that you can catch some of the fish but not others.

Fishing with Magnets

Data & Observations

Evaluate each animal for its ability to be caught. List the "eyes" as *brad* or *paper clip*. If you think that your magnet will catch the animal, mark a *Y* under the Prediction column. If you don't think it will be caught, mark *N*. Fish for the animals when you are done predicting. Then record your observations under the Results column. *Y* for yes and *N* for no.

Animal	"Eye"	Prediction	Result
Jellyfish			
Trout			
Eel			
Flounder			
Clam			
Salmon			
Sea Urchin			
Catfish			
Crab			
Shark			

How Come, Huh?

The paper clip is made up trillions of iron atoms, which are attracted to the magnet—the brass brad is not. When the magnet is lowered into the pool, you will only be able to catch the animals that are "attracted" to the bait.

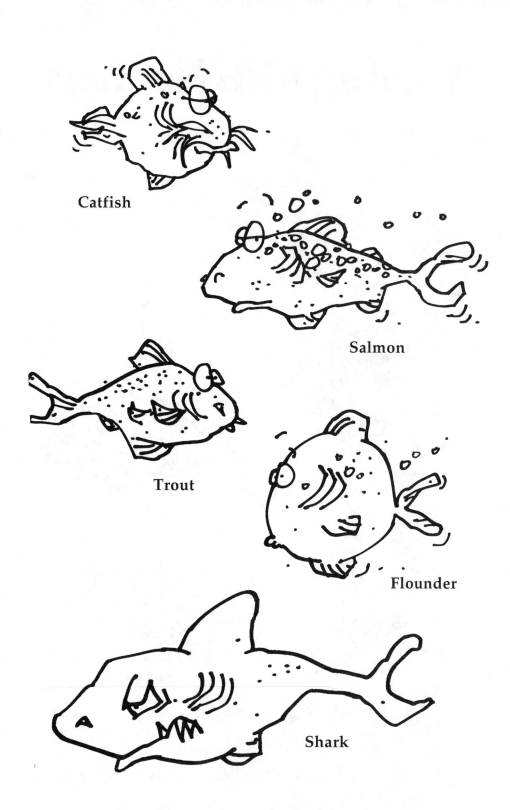

Catfish

Salmon

Trout

Flounder

Shark

Fishing with Magnets

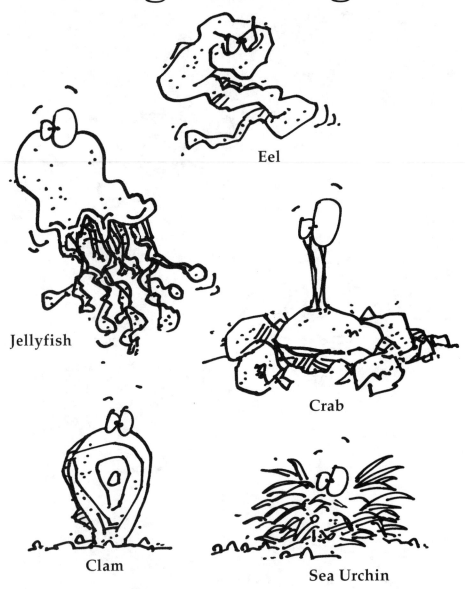

Eel

Jellyfish

Crab

Clam

Sea Urchin

Science Fair Extensions

23. Use different materials for the paper clips and brads.

24. Invent another game using magnets and materials that are attracted to magnets.

Iron, Salt, & Sand

The Experiment

To use your newly found knowledge of magnets, magnetic fields, and attraction, we present the following challenge for you to solve.

Create a mixture of salt, sand, and iron by pouring equal amounts of all three together on a piece of paper. Separate the iron from the remainder of the mixture, completely, in 10 seconds or less. Once that is accomplished, then separate the salt from the sand in the same amount of time. Good luck.

Materials

1   Piece of paper
1   Saltshaker
1   Bottle of iron filings
1   Box of sand
1   Bar magnet
1   Baggie
2   5-oz. Wax cup
1   Craft stick
1   Pie tin
     Water

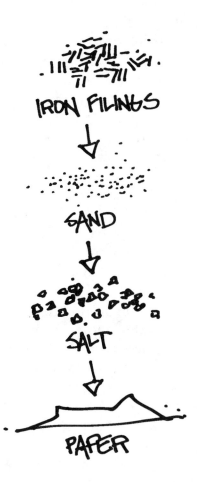

IRON FILINGS

SAND

SALT

PAPER

Procedure

1. Place the paper on the table in front of you and screw the cap off the saltshaker. Pour enough salt to cover a quarter and then add the same amount of iron filings. Finally, add an equivalent amount of sand to the iron-filing-and-salt mixture. Pick the paper up and tip it back and forth until all three compounds are mixed thoroughly.

Iron, Salt, & Sand

Procedure

2. To separate the iron filings from the sand and salt in less than 10 seconds is the next task. Place the magnet in the baggie. This procedure will keep the magnet from getting attached to the iron filings, and you will have a clean magnet at the end of the experiment. Once the magnet is in the baggie, run it around in the mixture of iron, sand, and salt on the paper. You will immediately observe that the iron filings are attracted to the magnet, but the salt and sand crystals are not. When you are done, simply return the filings to the container and toss the salt and sand in a cup.

3. Once the sand and the salt are in the cup, add water and take the craft stick and stir. Pour the water out into a second cup and the sand into a pie tin. You have now separated the salt from the sand. Congratulations you accomplished both tasks in the allotted amount of time—10 seconds or less.

4. Finally, to prove that the separations were complete take the salty water and pour it into the clean pie tin. Place the pie tin someplace where it will remain undisturbed for a day or two. Check the pie tin after 24 hours. You should notice that there are small crystals of salt starting to form on the edge of the pie tin.

How Come, Huh?

When you added the salt to the iron filings and the sand, you were creating a mixture. All three of those things were hanging out together, but they were not connected to one another. As you know from your previous labs, objects containing iron are attracted to magnets but sand (glass) and salt are not. When you ran the magnet through the mixture, the iron filings were immediately attracted to and lifted up by the magnet. This removed the iron filings in the requisite 10 seconds, but you still had a mixture of salt and sand to contend with.

By adding the salt and sand to the water, you were taking advantage of a characteristic of salt—it dissolves in water—whereas, sand does not. The salt dissolves into the water, which is poured off into the cup, and the sand is left behind and with time to spare. To prove that the salt was dissolved in the water, you allowed it to evaporate, forming salt crystals on the pie tin. What a great topic this is to study.

Science Fair Extensions

25. A fun zinger that you can throw at your friends, and amaze and astound your colleagues all at the same time is to take a package of dehydrated, iron-fortified cereal and expose this nutritional impostor.

The iron in the cereal is real, honest-to-Pete iron filings—not a chelated form usable by the body but real iron, just as good for you as if you were to suck on a nail. Tear open the package of Cream of Wheat and dip the magnet in the cereal. When you pull it out, you are going to have a bearded magnet.

Big Idea 4

Magnets are surrounded by an invisible magnetic field that can pass through materials that are permeable. Materials that do not allow the magnetic field to pass through them are called nonpermeable.

Opposites Attract • B. K. Hixson

Invisible Fingers

The Experiment

We know that some things containing iron are attracted to magnets but that most things are not. We also now know that magnets can be used to quickly separate some items from others.

The next challenge for you is to prove that even though most items are not attracted to magnets, the magnetic field can pass through those items and still attract other iron objects. In the words of those who write comic books, the magnetic field is made of super-penetrating lines of force that will not be stopped by wood, plastic, paper, cloth, or . . . even metal?

Materials

15 Paper clips, small
1   Baggie, plastic
1   Paper bag
1   Wood craft stick
1   Piece of fabric, cheesecloth
1   Iron saucepan
1   Cow magnet

Procedure

1. Scatter 15 paper clips on the table top and dip the plastic baggie into the pile. Record the number of paper clips that are picked up by the baggie in the data table on the next page. Does the baggie have a magnetic field? Unless there is a new brand on the market, probably not.

Invisible Fingers

2. Repeat the procedure above with the paper, wood sticks, fabric, and iron saucepan. Record all of your observations in the second column, Magnetic?, in the data table below. If it attracted the paper clips, write a *Y* and if it did not, mark a *N*. Write the number of paper clips that were attracted to the object without the magnet in the third column.

3. Open the plastic baggie and drop the cow magnet inside. Scatter 15 paper clips on the table top and dip the magnet into the pile. Record your observations in the fourth column of the data table below. Repeat this procedure placing the magnet in or between each of the items in the data table, and see if the magnetic field of the cow magnet can penetrate that item and collect paper clips.

Data & Observations

Record the number of paper clips that are attracted by each type of material and *through* each type of material.

Item Tested	Magnetic? Y/N	# Paper clips w/o magnet	# Paper clips w/magnet
Plastic			
Paper			
Wood			
Fabric			
Saucepan			

Opposites Attract • B. K. Hixson

How Come, Huh?

Scientists are not really sure just exactly what a magnetic field is, but we can detect its presence by using iron objects, compasses, and iron filings, among other things. We do know that magnetic fields can and do pass right through most objects, unless that object is made of iron.

Apparently when a magnetic field comes in contact with an object that contains lots of iron, the magnetic field is interrupted. It may wrap itself around the iron atoms in the object and pull it toward the magnet, which would account for the attraction. In that case the magnetic field does not pass beyond the iron object it encounters because it is essentially rerouted back to the magnet. Our example of this is the iron saucepan. The magnet inside the pot extends a magnetic field to the iron in the pot and then it gets rerouted back to the magnet, never having a chance to attract the paper clips.

Science Fair Extensions

26. Expand your tests and add Styrofoam, clay, rock, glass, ceramics, and any other material that you would like to test.

27. Design an experiment that allows you to test the "reach" of a magnetic field. Determine how far a magnet will influence an iron object, like a paper clip, and then add materials between the magnet. For example add wooden craft sticks, one at a time, until the magnet can no longer attract the paper clip. Measure that distance at the point where the influence is lost. Compare it with other materials.

28. We know that iron does not work. Design an experiment that allows you to test other metals. Try aluminum, copper, brass, and other metals that you can find in hardware stores.

Flying Paper Clips

The Experiment

Another challenge for you to ponder. Make a paper clip float in the middle of the air. In fact, Fi Ling says that if you solve this problem you will create an illusion of a paper clip flying away from the ground, restrained only by a thin thread.

Materials

1   Length of thread, 2 feet or so
1   Paper clip, small
1   Chair
1   Cow magnet
1   Table
1   Bar magnet
1   Piece of masking tape, 2 inches
1   Pair of scissors
1   Metric ruler

Procedure

1. Tie one end of the thread to the paper clip. Tape the other end of the thread to the seat of the chair.

2. Balance the cow magnet so that one end sticks over the edge of the table.

3. Hold the paper clip up and slide the chair toward the cow magnet until the magnetic field of the cow magnet is strong enough to attract the paper clip.

4. Release the paper clip and it will appear to levitate in midair. If you don't get it right away, change the angle that the paper clip flies, making it steeper. Or, you can try getting the paper clip very close but not touching the magnet. Play with the idea and have fun.

5. When you get the paper clip to fly, fill in the data table below. Then repeat the experiment using a bar magnet (or magnet of your choice) and fill out the data table.

Data & Observations
When you get the paper clip to fly, record the exact measurements that you used to get this experiment to work.

Length of string _____ cm
Distance of paper clip from *cow* magnet _____ cm

Length of string _____ cm
Distance of paper clip from *bar* magnet _____ cm

How Come, Huh?
The magnetic field of the magnet extends well beyond the physical border of the iron. This magnetic field reaches out and attracts the iron particles in the paper clip. The attraction is strong enough to overcome the force of gravity, and the mass of the paper clip being pulled toward the Earth, so it appears that the paper clip is flying.

Science Fair Extensions
29. Add paper clips to the experiment. See if you can get two, three, four, or more paper clips on their own individual strings, flying toward the same magnet.

30. Fill a small baggie with iron filings and see if you can re-create this experiment.

The Magnet Regatta

The Experiment

So far in this section we have experimented and proven that the magnetic field can pass through air and a variety of solid materials. Next up we are going to experiment with our own personal puddle of water.

When you are done with this lab, you will not only have entertained yourself, but you will have also proven, conclusively, that magnetic fields can travel through water.

Materials

1	4" x 4" Cork square
1	Pencil
1	Pair of scissors
1	4" x 4" Paper square
2	Pins
2	Steel thumbtacks
1	Shallow baking dish
4	Large books
2	Magnet wands
	Water

Procedure

1. Using the top pattern to the right as a guide, draw two boat bottoms on the piece of cork and cut them out.

2. Using the middle pattern to the right as a guide, draw two boat sails on the piece of paper and cut them out.

3. Assemble your boat. Place the pin in the sail using the bottom illustration as a guide, and then pin the sail into the cork bottom.

4. Now, add the steel thumbtack to the bottom of the boat, and voila, you are now officially a boat builder.

5. Fill the baking dish half full with water and balance it on top of four large books that have been spaced evenly in two piles of two from one another. Use the illustration above to get a general idea of how to set it up. Feel free to use your imagination.

6. Place the two boats in the water and, using the magnet wands, guide them around your pond using the magnetic field as your source of propulsion.

How Come, Huh?

The magnetic field of the wand magnet is able to pass through the glass dish and the water to attract the steel thumbtack on the bottom of the boat. As the magnet moves, the boat follows.

Science Fair Extensions

31. Have a contest to design the fastest boat. Do more thumbtacks make a difference? How about the design of the hull of the boat itself? Turn you imagination loose.

Magnetic Shielding

The Experiment

You know that magnetic fields can pass through a number of materials—but not metal items that contain iron. Engineers and scientists use this little tidbit of information to design machinery and protect sensitive instruments from the effects of magnetic fields by incorporating what is called magnetic shielding in their designs.

This idea, which we borrowed from our friends at the Exploratorium in San Francisco, demonstrates how magnetic shielding can be used to protect sensitive equipment from being exposed to a magnetic field.

Materials

2   Pieces of cardboard, 5 cm by 7 cm
2   Pencils
3   Rubber bands
1   Roll of masking tape
2   Donut magnets
6   Paper clips
1   Tongue depressor
1   Butter knife, iron

Procedure

1. Place the first piece of cardboard in front of you and position one pencil on either edge of the cardboard. Tape the pencils in place. Use the illustration on page 75 as a guide.

2. Place the second piece of cardboard on top of the first and rubber band the two pieces together to form a pencil sandwich. Check the second illustration below to see how you are doing.

3. Rubber band the two magnets to the top of your pencil sandwich and you are now ready to experiment.

4. Hold the pencil sandwich, magnet side up, over the paper clips. One at a time lift the paper clips up and stick them to the bottom of the sandwich. You will notice that they hang there and even space themselves out evenly. It's a territory thing.

5. Still keeping those paper clips hanging, insert the tongue depressor in the slot that has been created by the pencils. This positions the stick between the magnets and the paper clips. Gently wiggle the stick and notice what, if anything, happens to the paper clips.

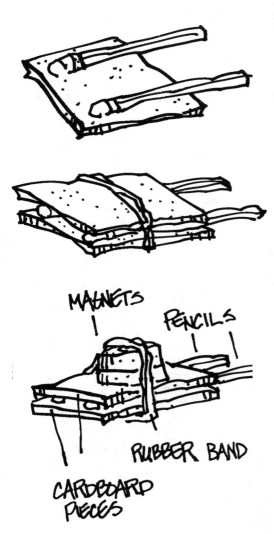

MAGNETS

PENCILS

RUBBER BAND

CARDBOARD PIECES

Magnetic Shielding

6. Remove the tongue depressor and insert the butter knife. Keep those paper clips hanging. Gently wiggle the butter knife back and forth and slide it around. Observe what happens to the paper clips as the butter knife interferes with the magnetic field produced by the magnets.

Data & Observations

1. Describe what happens when the tongue depressor is inserted in the sandwich?_____

_____

2. Describe what happens when the butter knife is inserted in

the sandwich? _____

_____

How Come, Huh?

The magnet produces a magnetic field that, as you know, zips right on through a lot of different kinds of materials. When you measure the ability of a magnetic field to pass through an object, it is called *reluctance*. Like electricity, magnetic fields take the easiest route—or the path of least reluctance—when they are zipping around the environment.

We show the magnetic lines of force as arrows radiating out from, and back to, the magnet. As you can see, the lines of force zing right through the permeable materials—cardboard and air—and head right on back to the magnet.

When you slid the tongue depressor in between the pieces of cardboard, it was no surprise that the paper clips did not fall off. They were still feeling the influence of the magnetic field of the magnets. Materials that allow magnetic fields to pass through them are called *permeable* materials. Cardboard, air, and wood all fall into this category.

When you inserted the butter knife, the iron in the knife provided a path of least reluctance and collected the lines of force from the magnetic field, detoured them down the length of the knife, and emptied them back out so they could re-enter the magnet. When this happened, the paper clips could no longer feel the effect of the magnetic field because they were being shielded from it by the butter knife, so they fell off. Materials that do not allow magnetic fields to pass through them are called *nonpermeable* materials and being mere peons in the vastly intellectual and terribly proper world of electromagnetic physics, we defer.

Science Fair Extensions

32. Find five other objects that will produce the same magnetic-shielding effect as the butter knife.

To Permeate or Not

The Experiment

That is the question, thank you, Mr. Shakespeare. We are going to introduce you to a magnetic fluid, called Ferrofluid that is used to enhance the performance of audio speakers, produce entertaining physics demonstrations, and coat the surfaces of far too many products to list in this paragraph and retain your interest.

Ferrofluid is a colloid; this means it has lots of tiny particles that remain dispersed in a solution without either dissolving or clumping together and that respond to magnetic fields. When there is no magnetic field, they just hang out and look terribly uninteresting. When you introduce a magnetic field, the particles in the Ferrofluid automatically take on the shape and direction of the magnetic field. We are going to use it to expand on the idea of magnetic shielding and how nonpermeable and permeable materials affect the magnetic field lines of force.

Materials

1   Tube with Ferrofluid
1   Donut magnet
1   Tongue depressor, wooden
1   Stainless steel spoon, big

Procedure

1. Hold the tube upright, like the cartoon above, and take a peek at the bluish-black sludge that is resting on the bottom of the tube. Say hello to Ferrofluid, a magnetically responsive colloid.

2. Now take the donut magnet and tipping the tube so it is parallel to the ground, slowly bring the magnet up to the tube, watching the Ferrofluid as you do. Draw pictures of what you see in the spaces provided in the Data & Observations section.

3. Now hold a tongue depressor between the tube and the magnet and observe what happens to the Ferrofluid. Compare this with inserting the tongue depressor into the cardboard sleeve from the previous experiment.

4. Put the tongue depressor down and put a stainless steel spoon between the tube and the magnet, then observe what happens to the Ferrofluid. Compare this with inserting the butter knife into the cardboard sleeve.

Data & Observations

Draw a picture of what the Ferrofluid looked like when the donut magnet was brought up toward the tube in the positions below and on page 80.

How Come, Huh?

The magnet produces a magnetic field that extends from the north and south poles. As the magnet is brought near the Ferrofluid, the particles in the fluid are attracted by, and align with, the magnetic lines of force in the magnet. Those are the little cones that you see sticking up on the bottom of the tube.

no magnet

To Permeate or Not

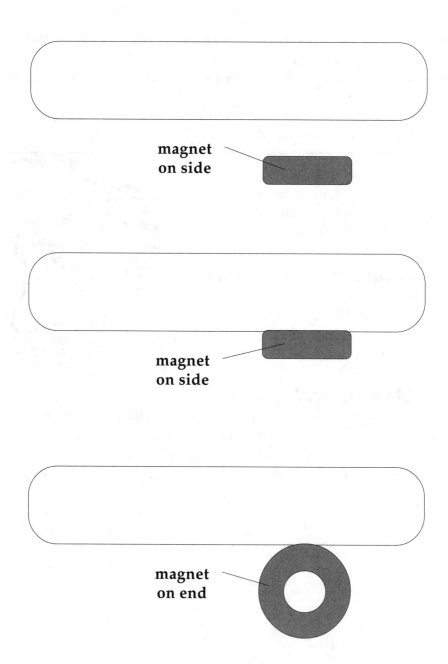

magnet on side

magnet on side

magnet on end

How Come, Huh?

If you insert the tongue depressor between the magnet and the Ferrofluid, nothing happens because the wood is a permeable material and does not interfere with the magnetic field. The spoon, however, is nonpermeable and does re-route the magnetic field of the magnet. This is why the cones of Ferrofluid flatten out or disappear. Another demonstration of magnetic shielding—we have just substituted Ferrofluid for paper clips.

Science Fair Extensions

33. Locate, predict, test, and verify five materials that are permeable and five that are nonpermeable.

34. You have demonstrated magnetic shielding using paper clips and Ferrofluid. Design an experiment that allows you to substitute iron filings for those two and still demonstrate the effects of magnetic shielding.

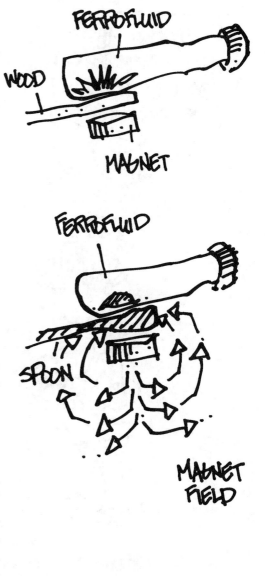

Big Idea 5

A compass is a tool used to detect magnetic fields. Magnetic fields can also be detected using iron filings.

The Magnet Detector

The Experiment

We know that certain items are magnetic but that most are not. We know that magnetic items produce an invisible magnetic field that extends out from the magnetic item and can even go through many kinds of material—but not iron. We also know that the Earth is a giant magnet having a North and South Pole that produce a giant magnetic field that covers the whole Earth and extends out into space.

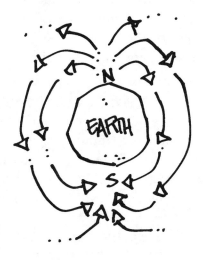

The interesting thing is that ancient ship navigators have discovered a tool, called a compass, that allows scientists to detect magnetic fields—the big one surrounding the Earth as well as smaller magnetic fields like the one that is produced by the magnets on your fridge. Your challenge is to learn to use the compass to detect the presence of magnetic fields in a variety of objects. Again, not all objects will produce a magnetic field, it is up to you to identify, predict, and test each item on your list.

Materials

1	Compass
1	16-Penny nail, ungalvanized
1	Large paper clip
1	Plastic straw
1	Wooden craft stick
1	Brass brad
1	Plastic pipette, 1 mL
1	Cow magnet
1	Rectangular magnet
2	Items of your choice

The Magnet Detector

Procedure

Hold the compass level in the palm of your hand. Test each item by bringing it near the compass. If the needle deflects, or moves toward, the item you are holding in your other hand, that item is producing a magnetic field.

Data & Observations

Evaluate each item before you test it with the compass. Predict if you think that the compass will detect a magnetic field. Use Y for yes and N for no. Then test the item and record the response that you observed with Y for yes and N for no. Add two items of your choice to the list and test them also.

Item Tested	Prediction	Compass Response
1. 16-Penny nail		
2. Large paper clip		
3. Plastic straw		
4. Wooden craft stick		
5. Brass brad		
6. Plastic pipette, 1 mL		
7. Cow magnet		
8. Rectangular magnet		
9.		
10.		

How Come, Huh?

You probably noticed that the items made from anything but iron did not have any effect on the compass you were holding. The reason for this is that iron objects have their iron atoms organized or lined up to produce a magnetic field. It is not very common for this to happen, but when it does, the magnetic field can be detected by a variety of items including another magnet, iron filings, or a compass. The other items do not produce a magnetic field, so there is no response from the compass.

The reason the compass works in the presence of iron is that the compass needle is actually a little, skinny magnet perched on a needle so that it is free to swing around. When a magnetic field is brought near a compass, the needle responds by pointing its opposite pole in the direction of the magnetic field.

Science Fair Extensions

35. Head back to the lab titled, What Is Magnetic?, pages 52–57, and test all of the materials in each of the data tables to create a more definitive argument for what attracts a compass.

36. Make a compass of your own and repeat the experiment using your homemade version. Tie a piece of string around a bar magnet and then hang it so it spins freely. Test each of the items on your list using your homemade compass and compare that with your compass findings.

37. Create a game where 10 items are inside paper bags. The contestants must test each item without opening the bag and determine if it is magnetic or not.

The Iron-Pot Prison

The Experiment

If the Earth is one, giant magnet producing a very large magnetic field that extends all the way out into space, it stands to reason that this magnetic field is also subject to the same kinds of interruptions and shielding that smaller magnets experience.

This lab allows you demonstrate that an iron pot will shield a compass from the magnetic field of the Earth.

Materials

1   Compass
1   Wooden bowl
1   Iron pot

Procedure

1. Place the compass on the table and note the direction of the needle.

2. Now place the compass in a wooden bowl and note the direction of the needle.

3. Finally, place the compass in an iron pot and notice the direction of the needle.

How Come, Huh?

The iron particles in the pot are nonpermeable and therefore shield the compass from the lines of force from the Earth's magnetic field.

Science Fair Extensions

38.   Try containers made out of a variety of materials—Styrofoam, plastic, aluminum, and fabric for starters.

Magnetic Field Mapping

The Experiment

You can "see" the magnetic field that surrounds a magnet using three different tools. The first is a compass, which will align with the lines of forces radiating out from the poles of the magnet. Second, would be the Ferrofluid. Third are iron filings that also align with the lines of force but form a picture of the field much more quickly. We will save that lab for the next lesson.

According to the musings of many scientists you cannot only detect but also "see" the magnetic field that surrounds magnets using a compass. They contend that the reason this is possible is because the compass needle will align with the lines of forces radiating out from the poles of the magnet when it is placed next to or near the magnet. By moving the compass around the magnet and recording the position of the compass needle you will be able to infer, or figure out, the direction of the magnetic field surrounding any magnet. Or at least we think so . . .

Materials

1   Cow magnet
1   Pencil
1   Sheet of paper
1   Compass
1   Donut magnet

Procedure

1. Using the page setup on page 89, put the cow magnet in the middle of the paper. Take your pencil and trace around the outside of it. Now, noticing the outline of the compass, you will see a pattern of circles immediately around the magnet border and then another set around that.

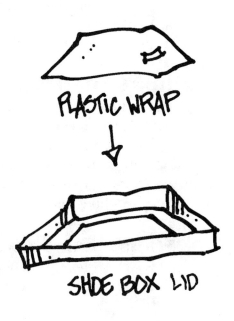

PLASTIC WRAP

SHOE BOX LID

Magnetic Field Mapping

2. Place the compass on each of the spots next to the magnet, look at the position of the compass needle, and draw an arrow showing which way the north and south ends of the compass are pointing.

3. Move the compass out to the second set of circles and repeat this procedure. When you are all done, connect the lines showing the needle position for each of the three markings, and you should have a pretty good idea of what the magnetic lines of force look like. If you have time, do the same thing with the donut magnet using page 90. You will find that your results are slightly different—something we are sure that you will want to discuss with an adult.

4. When you are all done, connect the lines showing the needle position for each of the markings, and you should have a pretty good idea of what the magnetic lines of force look like.

Data & Observations

The next two pages are provided for you to map the magnetic fields of a cow magnet and a donut magnet (which should be a pleasant surprize) by tracing the position of the compass needle.

How Come, Huh?

The compass is influenced by the lines of force radiating from the magnet. As the lines of force bend, the compass will align to reflect this force. By mapping the position of the needle at various spots around the magnet, you are plotting data points. By connecting the needles points, you will get a rough picture of what the magnetic field looks like. To refine this we use iron filings in the next lab.

Science Fair Extensions

39. Get a larger chunk of paper and see how far out you have to go before the magnetic field becomes undetectable and the Earth's magnetic field takes over. Try it with different magnets.

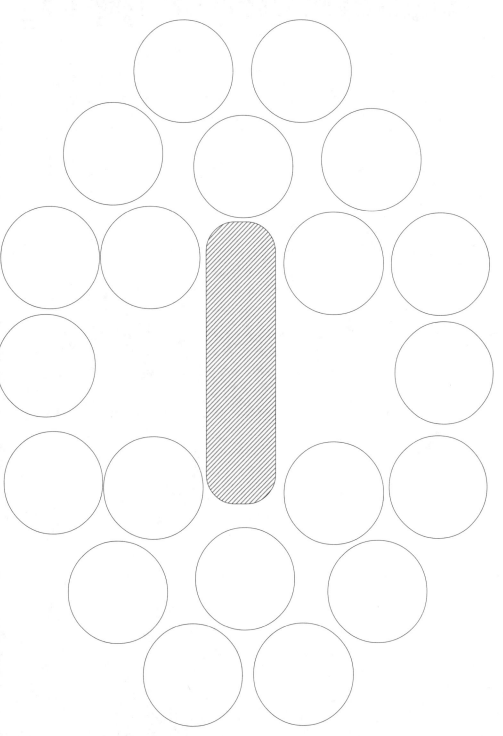

Magnetic Field Mapping

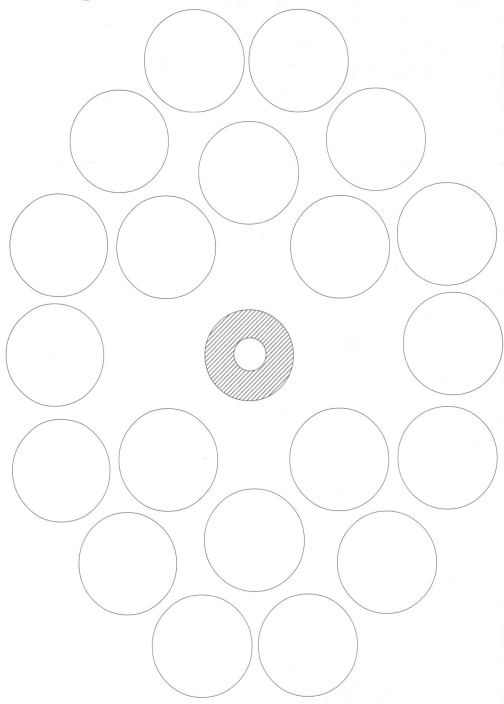

Iron-Filing Maps

The Experiment

The compass allows you to detect the magnetic field of the magnet and see where those lines of force are pointing, but it does not really give you the whole picture. To actually see the entire magnetic field you would either need a huge pile of very small compasses or the next best thing, a pile of iron filings.

This lab will allow you create a picture of the magnetic field surrounding three different magnets by using a thin layer of iron filings.

Materials

1   Bottle of iron filings
1   Shoe box lid
1   Pair of scissors
1   Sheet of plastic wrap
1   Roll of tape
1   Donut magnet
1   Cow magnet
1   Magnetic wand
1   Bar magnet
1   Pencil

Procedure

1. To make your magnetic field viewer begin by cutting the center from the lid of the shoe box. Flip the shoe box lid upside down and place a square of plastic wrap on the inside of the lid and tape it in place. Flip the shoe box lid over and you are ready to go.

Iron-Filing Maps

2. Place a magnet under the shoe box lid, centering it in the plastic wrap window. Once the magnet is centered, sprinkle iron filings all over the top of the shoe box lid. Be generous; you will be able to recycle them.

3. Once you have the filings on the lid, gently tap the edge of the box and the filings will align in the natural pattern of the lines of force.

4. Draw a picture of the magnetic field for each of the three magnets on separate sheets of paper.

5. Notice that the general direction of the compass needles that you recorded by drawing in the previous lab and the pattern and direction of the iron filings should be very similar to one another.

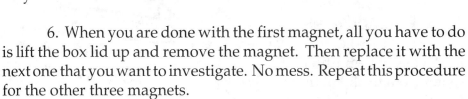

6. When you are done with the first magnet, all you have to do is lift the box lid up and remove the magnet. Then replace it with the next one that you want to investigate. No mess. Repeat this procedure for the other three magnets.

Data & Observations

On a separate sheet of paper, draw a picture of the magnetic field of the cow magnet. Then trace the outline of the next magnet that you are experimenting with and then draw the magnetic field as revealed by the iron filings. Replicate the magnetic field around the cow magnet in the space on a separate sheet of paper.

How Come, Huh?

Each iron filing is a miniature magnet or compass, with a north and south pole. The magnet influences the filings, and they move to reflect the lines of force coming from the magnet. By tapping on the edge of the box you are simply aligning the iron filings along the pathways created by the magnetic field.

The cow magnet should have created magnetic field patterns. The donut magnet is another creature all together. It is created by taking a long tube magnet and slicing it like a loaf of bread. Since the magnet has already been generated when the slicing takes place, this leaves a north pole on one side of the magnet and a south pole on the other side of the magnet. When you lay it on top of the paper, you are literally taking an end view of the top of the magnet—not a side view like you were with the other magnets.

Science Fair Extensions

40. There are several magnets that we have left uninvited to the party. Try horseshoe magnets, book magnets, bar magnets, disc magnets, and lodestone for starters.

3-D Magnetic Fields

The Experiment

Most of the time folks see magnetic fields as flat, two-dimensional configurations when in actuality they are three-dimensional. Spend some time playing with the Ferrofluid and you will figure that out right away. The problem is that the way we look at magnets most of the time does not allow us to see all three dimensions. We are going to change that with this lab.

We are going to incorporate a very strong magnet used by cattle ranchers called a cow magnet. It is inserted into the first stomach of range cattle. That way when these silly animals eat barbed wire and old tin cans the metal stays in the first stomach and does not pass through the system causing bleeding.

Materials

1   Bottle of iron filings
1   Clear, clean, 16-oz. bottle
1   Cow magnet
1   Plastic test tube
1   Bicycle-tube section, 3"
1   Rubber band

Procedure

1. Pop the lid on the iron-filing shaker and empty about half the bottle into the pop bottle that you have previously checked to make sure it is clean and dry.

2. Slide the cow magnet into the plastic test tube. Make sure that it slides all the way to the end.

3. Place one end of the bicycle-tube section over the plastic test tube. Slide the tube inside the bottle and fold the other end of the bicycle tube over the mouth of the bottle.

This will enclose the bottle and keep the iron filings from flying all over the place. Use the illustration to the right as a guide.

4. When you are ready, give the bottle a couple of good shakes. This will toss the iron filings up into the air, and they will come in contact with the magnetic field of the cow magnet. As the iron filings stick to the test tube, a three-dimensional picture of the magnetic field will appear. Pay special attention to the concentration of filings near the poles as well as to the orientation of the iron filings near the middle. This clearly demonstrates that the strength of the magnet is in the poles.

5. When it is time to clean up, simply lift the magnet gently up toward the mouth of the bottle and roll the bicycle-tube section back. When the magnet is completely out of the bicycle-tube section, the iron filings will fall back into the bottle.

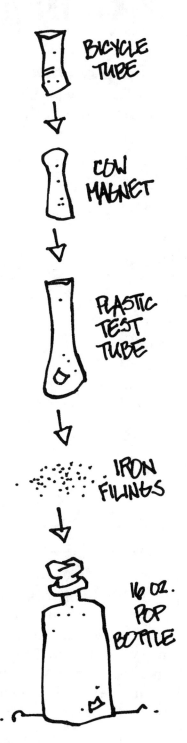

BICYCLE TUBE

COW MAGNET

PLASTIC TEST TUBE

IRON FILINGS

16 OZ. POP BOTTLE

3-D Magnetic Fields

Data & Observations

In the space provided below draw a picture of what a three-dimensional magnetic field for a cow magnet looks like.

How Come, Huh?

The cow magnet has a very strong magnetic field. As the iron filings are tossed around the inside of the bottle, they are attracted to the magnetic field that radiates out from the magnet. Because the filings are small and can be influenced to move in any direction, they align with the lines of force and create a three-dimensional picture of the magnetic field.

Opposites Attract • B. K. Hixson

Big Idea 6

The Earth is a giant magnet with a North Pole and a South Pole. A magnetic field surrounds the Earth.

Compass in a Cup

The Experiment

With just a couple of simple materials you will be able to turn an ordinary drinking cup into a compass. Will miracles ever cease?

Materials

1   Piece of index card
1   Pair of scissors
1   Needle, steel, sewing
1   Thread, 12 inches
1   Pencil
1   Drinking glass
1   Bar magnet
1   Compass

Procedure

1. Cut a one-inch square from the index card. Fold it in half and, using the needle, pierce a small hole in the center of the fold.

2. Wiggle one end of the thread through the hole. Double knot the other end and gently pull it up to the hole.

3. Tie the loose end of the thread around the middle of the pencil. Hold the index card in the drinking glass and wind the thread up so that the card is in the middle, hanging freely in the glass, see page 99.

PENCIL

THREAD —

CARD

4.   Stroke the sewing needle with the north end of the bar magnet about 50 times. We use the word *stroke* instead of *rub* because it is important that you lift the magnet up at the end of each stroke and place it back at the top of the needle.

Think of combing your hair. You would not stick your comb or brush on your head and run it back and forth. You comb or brush in one direction to organize the hair shafts. You are doing the same thing with the iron particles in the needle.

5. Slide the needle into the card using the illustration to the right as a guide. Lower the card into the glass and let the needle orient with the magnetic field of the Earth.

Compare the position of your compass with the position of the needle on your commercially prepared compass.

How Come, Huh?

The iron particles in the needle were organized and lined up when you stroked the needle with the magnet. This magnetized the needle. When the needle was free to move in the cup, the magnetic field of the Earth influenced the needle and caused it to align with the North and South Poles of the Earth.

Science Fair Extensions

41. Fill the cup with water and try suspending the needle in that medium. Do you get the same results or does the water impede—or interfere with—the movement of the needle?

Floating Compass

The Experiment

With a little bit of physics know-how and absolutely no magic whatsoever, you are going to turn your breakfast cereal bowl into a compass.

This is not recommended as part of the daily diet but definitely a conversation starter.

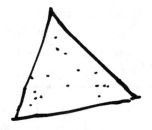

Materials

1   Bowl, cereal
1   Piece of cork
1   Pair of scissors
1   Paper clip
1   Bar magnet
1   Roll of masking tape
1   Compass
    Water

Procedure

1. Fill the bowl two-thirds full of water and set it aside.

2. Cut an arrow shape out of the cork using the top pattern above as a guide.

3. Stroke the paper clip with the north end of the bar magnet about 50 times. We use the word *stroke* instead of *rub* because it is important that you lift the magnet up at the end of each stroke and place it back at the top of the paper clip, just like in the previous lab.

4. Tape the paper clip to the center of the cork. Again, use the illustration to the left as a guide.

5. Place the cork in the center of the water in the cereal bowl. It will float and spin while the paper clip aligns with the magnetic field of the Earth.

How Come, Huh?

The iron particles in the paper clip were organized and lined up when you stroked it with the magnet. This magnetized the paper clip. When the paper clip was free to move in the water, the magnetic field of the Earth influenced the paper clip and caused it to align with the North and South Poles of the Earth.

Science Fair Extensions

42. You know that paper clips work. How about a sewing needle? A piece of iron wire? How many things can you find that you can convert into a floating compass?

43. Does the temperature of the water have any affect on how well this experiment works or how fast the compass needle aligns with the poles of the Earth?

44. Determine if the mass or shape of the cork has anything to do with the ability of the compass to respond to the poles of the Earth. Is there a material better suited to this job than cork?

Compass Wand

The Experiment
Enough with the compasses that take a lot of work to put together. Here is a very simple idea that can be used a variety of ways.

Materials
1 Wand magnet
1 Length of string, 18 in.
1 Roll of masking tape
1 Compass

Procedure
1. Tie the string to the center of the wand magnet so that it balances and swings freely.

2. Tape the other end of the string to the edge of the table. Let the magnet dangle freely.

3. When the magnet comes to a rest, compare the position of the magnet with the position of a compass needle.

How Come, Huh?
When the magnet was free to spin and move, the magnetic field of the Earth influenced the magnet and caused it to align with the North and South Poles of the Earth.

Science Fair Extensions
45. Re-create the experiment using different kinds of magnets: bar, disc, donut, as well as a piece of lodestone, if you have some available. Compare the ability of each magnet to line up in the Earth's magnetic field.

Big Idea 7

Some molecules have both positive and negative ends, like the poles of a magnet, and are called bipolar, or diamagnetic. This characteristic allows these tiny, building blocks to behave like magnets. Water is an excellent example.

Jumping Paper

The Experiment

Figure out a way of using magnetic attraction to get a piece of paper to either jump or be pulled into a drinking glass.

Materials

1   Sheet of paper
1   Pair of scissors
1   Drinking glass
    Water

Procedure

1. Cut a strip of paper 8 inches long and a half an inch wide.

2. Fold the paper into an accordion shape; use the illustration on the right as a guide. The folds should be about a half an inch apart. Be sure to bend the last fold of the paper, the one at the bottom, straight down so that it is pointing directly at the water in the glass.

3. Lower the last fold of the paper into the water and get it wet. Lift the paper out of the water and then lower it very slowly toward the surface again, *do not get it in the water*. What you will observe is that as you get closer and closer to the water, the paper eventually jumps or appears to be pulled quickly into the drinking glass.

4. Repeat the experiment and see how far you can get from the surface of the water in the glass and still have the paper jump into it.

How Come, Huh?

Being just like little magnets, water molecules are naturally attracted to one other. They have a positive end and a negative end just like a magnet. The hydrogen atoms on the top of the water molecule, the ones that look like Mickey Mouse ears, have a positive charge, or for the sake of the argument, act like the north end of a magnet. The much bigger oxygen atom at the bottom of the molecule has a negative charge and acts like the south end of a magnet. Because they have this shape, the water molecules are all attracted to one another and line up with positive hydrogen atoms attracted to the negative oxygen atoms, so they hang onto each other magnetically when they get close to one another.

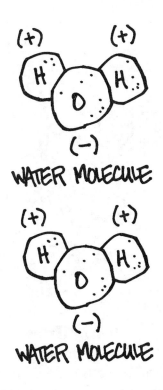

When the end of the paper is dipped into the water, the water molecules all line up inside the paper. As the paper is lowered toward the surface of the water, the water molecules in the glass start to feel the pull of the water molecules in the paper. When the paper gets close enough, the water molecules in the glass tug on the water molecules in the paper and pull them down into the water to be with their other water-molecule buddies.

Science Fair Extensions

46. Experiment to find out if the temperature of the water affects the speed of the reaction.

47. Change the shape of the paper somehow—make it thinner, thicker, add or subtract the number of folds—and see if the experiment is altered in any way.

Holey Cheesecloth

The Experiment

We will demonstrate that you can pour water through a piece of cheesecloth into a drinking glass, but that this same piece of cheesecloth will not let any water out of your drinking glass when it is turned upside down full of water.

Materials

2   Drinking glasses
1   Piece of cheesecloth
1   Rubber band
    Water

Procedure

1. Using an empty drinking glass, place the cheesecloth over the opening, pull it tight, and rubber band it in place.

2. Fill the other drinking glass with water and pour it directly into the first glass, through the cheesecloth, from a height of about 10 inches. You will notice that you have no trouble filling your drinking glass with water.

3. Holding your drinking glass over a sink or outside where you can make a mess, quickly flip the glass upside down with your hand on top of the cheesecloth. Slowly remove your hand and observe what happens to the water in the drinking glass.

How Come, Huh?

When you are pouring the water into the drinking glass, it has lots of energy. Starting out 10 inches above the drinking glass gives it lots of potential energy. As the water is pulled by gravity toward the glass covered with cheesecloth, it speeds up and has even more energy; so that when it hits the holes in the cheesecloth, it zips right on through and into the bottom of the container. That explains the first half of the experiment.

A couple of things happen in the second part of the experiment. First, as you flip the drinking glass upside down, your hand temporarily blocks the water from falling by holding it inside the container. This gives the water time to clog the holes in the cheesecloth, which it does because of that natural attraction between water molecules—it's that magnet thing that we presented in the first idea in this section. So the water molecules are hanging onto each other, plugging the holes in the cheesecloth. But we still don't know why the water doesn't come gushing out of the drinking glass when you remove your hand. This is because when you flip the drinking glass upside down, you are actually creating a partial vacuum at the top of the drinking glass—which means that there is less pressure in the top of the drinking glass than on the outside of it where the pressure is about 14.7 pounds per square inch.

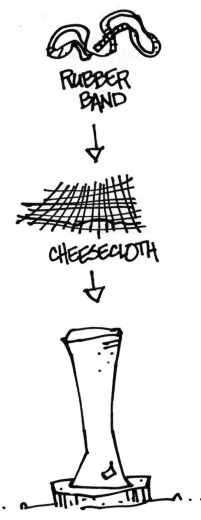

RUBBER BAND

CHEESECLOTH

Holey Cheesecloth

So here's the scenario: water plugging the holes of the cheese-cloth basically makes a single, uniform surface. A couple of pounds of water and a little bit of air pressure inside the drinking glass are pushing *down* on the cheesecloth, whereas 14.7 pounds per square inch of air pressure are pushing *up* on the cheesecloth. The water does not have enough weight or energy to push the cheesecloth out of the way so that it can escape.

Science Fair Extensions

48. Repeat this experiment using an index card in place of the cheesecloth and see if you can replicate the results.

49. Try other kinds of materials—cotton, silk, rayon, burlap—and see if you can duplicate the results that you got with the cheese-cloth. Compare the size of the holes in the fabric with the effectiveness of the fabric as a cloth that holds water and try to determine if that has anything at all to do with this experiment.

50. Substitute other liquids.

Bending Water

The Experiment

You can get a stream of water to wiggle and bend using a balloon that has been electrostatically charged.

Materials

1   Rubber balloon
1   Volunteer
1   Sink with water

Procedure

1. Rub the balloon on the head of a volunteer. As you rub, occasionally lift the balloon up off their hair about 6 inches. The hair will follow. After about 30 seconds of rubbing, the hair should be sticking up all around.

2. Start a thin stream of water trickling from the faucet. Bring the charged balloon near the stream of water and observe what happens to the water.

3. Move the charged balloon back and forth and get the stream of water to wiggle.

How Come, Huh?

Water molecules have a positive and a negative charge. As the water molecules fall in the stream of water, they are free to move around and rotate. When the negative charge of the balloon comes near the water, the positive end of the water molecules are attracted toward the balloon. Since the molecules like each other, they bring their buddies along for the visit too, which we call call cohesion— and everyone wiggles over to say hello.

Magnetic Soap Bubbles

The Experiment

A rubber balloon will be rubbed on someone's head, preferably someone with shoulder-length, fine hair. As the electrons gang up on the surface of the balloon, the hair will begin to wig out. You can also stick the balloon to the ceiling, walls, passing secretaries, or wool sweaters. The same balloon has a very interesting effect on soap bubbles that happen to be floating around the room.

Materials

1   Rubber balloon
1   Volunteer
    (The cat will also do in a pinch.)
1   Bottle of bubble solution

Procedure

1. Inflate the balloon. If this is hard to do, have someone lend you a lung.

2. Select a volunteer. For best results use someone who has shoulder-length hair that is free of mousse, hair spray, or gel. Fine hair tends to work better than coarse hair. This experiment works best on a dry day—the lower the humidity the better. And remember, blondes may have more fun, but not until you rub their heads.

Rub the balloon all over the volunteer's head. As you rub, occasionally lift the balloon up off the hair about 6 inches. The hair will follow. After about 30 seconds of rubbing, the hair should be sticking up all around.

3. Have another person blow a bubble. Hold the charged balloon near the soap bubbles and you will find that several of them will be attracted to the balloon. Select a bubble and you can tug it all over the classroom with the balloon.

How Come, Huh?

Opposite charges (negative and positive) attract, and like charges (negative and negative) or (positive and positive) repel, or drive apart. The balloon has a huge negative charge because it has stolen all these loose electrons. The hair has a huge positive charge because all of its electrons have been stolen. Balloon negative, hair positive; they attract. When you take the balloon out of the picture, the hair still tends to stand up on end. This is because each of the hair strands has a positive charge. Like charges repel, and since they can't stand each other, they get as far away from one another as possible. In this case, they stand on end.

The bubble is attracted to the static charge on the balloon because our water molecule has one side that is positively charged and one side that is negatively charged. Opposites attract.

Science Fair Extensions

51. There are lots of items that will hold an electrostatic charge. Experiment with rabbit fur, a fluorescent tube, a glass rod that has been charged with a piece of wool, and anything else that you think may attract soap bubbles.

Pinching Water

The Experiment

By now you should know that water molecules are very friendly with one another. They are great buddies and love to hang out together. In this experiment you are going to take two streams of water that are diverging, or going separate directions, and with a pinch of a couple of fingers, they will converge, or come together—until you flick them and they separate.

Materials

1   # 303 Soup can
1   Hammer
1   Nail, 16-penny
1   Roll of tape
1   Tub or sink
     Water

Procedure

1. Using the hammer and nail prepare two small holes near the bottom of the soup can.

The holes should be one-half inch from the bottom seam and one-half inch from each other. Use the illustration to the right as a guide.

2. Place a small piece of tape over the holes and fill the can with water.

3. Hold the can over the sink or tub and remove the tape from the holes. The water should start to empty out of the can through the two holes. You will notice that the two streams of water diverge or separate and go different directions. Take your thumb and forefinger and literally pinch the two streams of water together. When you remove your fingers the streams should be one.

4. The water should continue to flow as a single stream. To separate the streams of water simply give them a flick. Once they are separated, they stay separated.

How Come, Huh?

When you bring the water molecules from the two streams in contact with one another, they adhere, or stick, to one another forming a single stream. By pinching the water you are simply moving the streams of water molecules close enough together for them to be attracted to one another.

When you flick the single stream of water, you are literally separating the two streams, and they are just far enough apart that they cannot attract and hold one another.

Science Fair Extensions

52. It works with two streams, how about three? Four?

53. Determine the "tolerances" for hole placement. In other words, how far apart is too far and how close together is too close?

54. What happens if you place the holes on top of one another and the streams of water are lined up vertically instead of horizontally? Can you still pinch them together?

Pouring Water

The Experiment

It is entirely possible to pour a can full of water into another can. Big deal, you say? What if the two cans are positioned so they are two feet apart—horizontally.

Taking advantage of the attraction of water molecules for one another, we can actually pour a full can of water across a two-foot gap into another can and not spill too much in the process.

Materials

2   #303 Soup cans
1   String, cotton, 3 feet long
1   Volunteer
     Water

Procedure

1. Fill one of the two soup cans three-fourths full with water. Soak the string in the water.

2. Stretch the string from one can to the other, using the illustration on page 115 as a guide. Place the remainder of the string in the can that you will be filling with water.

3. Gently tip the can that is full of water so that it begins to run down the string. Work slowly, as this is not a fast process. As the water empties out of the can, it will run down the string and into the other can. Keep the water coming out of the can in a steady, uninterrupted stream.

4. When you get to the end of the water in the can, pull the string taut and let the rest of the water that was in the string run down into the second can. Congratulations, you have just poured a can of water sideways.

How Come, Huh?

The water molecules like to hang onto one another. This is called cohesion. The reason they like to stick to one another is that they are shaped like little magnets—with a positive top and a negative bottom. All of these little magnets line up and attract one another.

When you soaked the string, you filled the air spaces in the cotton string with water molecules. As the water in the can started down the string, the water molecules in the string provided an anchor, or support, as they slid down toward the other can.

Science Fair Extensions

55. Increase the horizontal distance between the two cans and see if you can find what the limits might be.

56. Substitute a cotton rope and a couple of 5-gallon buckets for the string and the soup cans. Could you get the experiment to work? Move up to the next larger scale and repeat the experiment.

Stacking Water Molecules

The Experiment

Start with a drinking glass completely full of water. We define "completely full" as when the water level is exactly even with the top of the drinking glass. Now it's time to figure out a way to add 50 paper clips to the drinking glass without spilling any water. There are two constraints, you cannot physically remove any of the water by spilling, drinking, or using an absorbent material. This would be a blatant violation of the creative process. Second, your time limit for completing this activity once you have received inspiration is a mere 10 minutes, so if you were planning on waiting for the water to evaporate, keep thinking, you just hit a dead end.

Materials

1   Drinking glass
1   Small cork
1   Box of paper clips
1   Plastic, 1 mL pipette
    Water

Procedure

1. Fill your drinking glass so that the water is perfectly level across the very top of it. Predict how many paper clips you will be able to add, and record that number in the space provided on the next page in the Data & Observations section.

2. Start carefully adding and counting paper clips. Don't stop until you add 50 or finally add one too many and the water in your drinking glass spills over onto the table. Record the number of paper clips that you added to achieve this glorious feat on a separate sheet of paper.

3. If you get to 50 and want to keep going, have at it. You may be surprised at the number of paper clips that you can actually get into the drinking glass.

Data & Observations

1. I predict that I will be able to add _____ paper clips to my drinking glass before it spills.

2. Keep track of the paper clips that you add on a separate sheet of paper.

How Come, Huh?

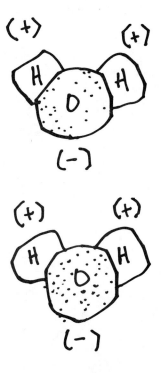

Every time you add a paper clip to the drinking glass it sinks to the bottom of your container. As it does this, it pushes up a tiny little bit of water exactly equal to its volume. After a couple of paper clips, this would normally spill some of the liquid out of the drinking glass and onto the table. But because water molecules are attracted to each other, a phenomena called cohesion, they hang onto their buddies if it looks like one of them might fall over the edge.

As more and more paper clips are added to the drinking glass, more and more water molecules are shoved up out of the container, above the rim. Alas, the water molecules are not easily intimidated or defeated, and in response to being displaced, they form a bulge—visual evidence of surface tension. This goes on for a while, the bulge growing with every paper clip that is added; but eventually the water molecules cannot hang on any longer and some of them take the plunge over the edge.

Stacking Water Molecules

Science Fair Extensions

57. Repeat the experiment with several other items—pennies, brads, bolts, nuts—and see if the result is the same or if this is just peculiar to paper clips. In fact, while you are at it, try adding more water to the container and see if you can create the bulge that way. Taking time to explore this extension will give you a leg up on the next experiment.

58. Try this same experiment with different solutions—not all liquid molecules are attracted as strongly to one another. Make a list of 10 common liquids and decide which ones have surface tension and which ones do not.

Centering a Cork

The Experiment

When a small cork is placed on the water in your drinking glass, it always migrates to the side of the cylinder. Despite several conversations and much consternation, you can never seem to get it to stay centered in the middle of the drinking glass and not touch the sides. Your task is to figure out a way to get it to stay in the middle without having anything physically hold it in place other than water and air.

Materials

1   Drinking glass
1   Small cork
1   Paper clips, box
1   Pipette, plastic, 1 mL
     Water

Procedure

1. To set this challenge up you are going to want to fill your drinking glass almost all the way to the top with water. Place the cork in the center of the drinking glass, and you will notice that it migrates or moves to the side of the drinking glass almost immediately. Push the cork back to the center of the drinking glass, let go, and it wanders back to the side—very uncooperative.

Centering a Cork

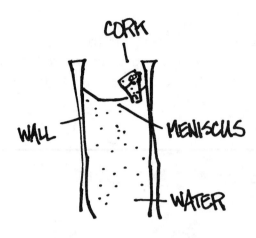

2. One way to remedy this problem is to slowly add paper clips to the drinking glass until you start to form a bulge at the top—caused by all of the little water magnets hanging onto one another. When the bulge in the water starts to appear, you will notice that the cork begins to float to the highest point in the water, which is the top of the bulge and, coincidentally, the center of the drinking glass. Mission accomplished.

3. Time for round two. Not wanting to be left with only one solution to the challenge, empty the paper clips, refill the water, and replace the cork.

Using the plastic pipette, slowly add water instead of paper clips to the drinking glass. As you do this, you will notice that the cohesion (that magnetic attraction we talked about) of the water molecules starts to create a bulge again, just like with the paper clips. As you keep adding the water, you will notice that the cork, which likes to float to the "highest" point in the water, will eventually be floating in the middle of the container directly on top of the bulge created by the surface tension in the water.

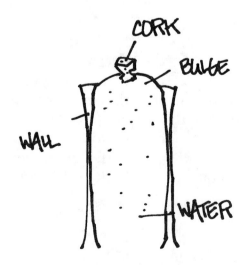

How Come, Huh?

Being less dense than water, the cork will always float to the highest point. When the water level is below the rim of the drinking glass, the water forms a dip, called a meniscus (men • iss • cuss), inside the container. With a meniscus the highest point of the water in the container is along the perimeter of the container so the cork always migrates to the side.

By adding paper clips or more water—both of which displace the water beyond the capacity of the drinking glass, a dome of water is formed creating a high point in the water. The cork will always float to the highest point in the water, so it heads to the top of the dome, which is also in the middle of the drinking glass. You've just figured out another challenge.

Science Fair Extensions

59. Predict if this experiment will work with a liquid that does not have surface as strong as tension, and then perform the experiment to support your hypothesis.

60. Try the experiment with other objects that float and see if you get the same results. Now that we think of it maybe you could try a drop of vegetable oil.

Big Idea 8

Magnets have a north pole and a south pole; like poles repel and opposite poles attract. Magnetic fields are strongest at the poles.

Magnet Strength

The Experiment

The first question we need to address is where the strength of a magnet lies. Are magnets strongest at the poles as we have proposed, or are they strongest in the middle? Then again perhaps the strength of a magnet is evenly dispersed throughout the design? There is one way to find out—nab your magnets and come along.

Materials

1   Bar magnet
1   Cow magnet
1   Horseshoe magnet
1   Box of straight pins

Procedure

1.   Imagine the bar magnet being divided up in to five equal sections: north pole, north middle, middle, south middle, and south pole.

2.   Holding the north pole of the magnet in your hand, add as many pins to the south pole as it will possibly support. Record that number in the Data & Observations section.

3. Remove the pins from the south pole of the magnet and start to add as many pins to the south middle section of the magnet as it will support. When no more will hang off the magnet, record that number in the Data & Observations section.

4.   Repeat this procedure for the middle, north middle, and north poles of the magnet. When you have completed testing the bar magnet, substitute a cow magnet, and then a horseshoe magnet, and see if your test results vary.

Magnet Strength

Data & Observations

Record the maximum number of pins that you were able to hang off each section of the magnet in the boxes provided.

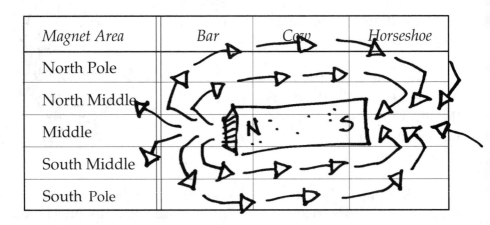

Magnet Area	Bar	Cow	Horseshoe
North Pole			
North Middle			
Middle			
South Middle			
South Pole			

How Come, Huh?

The magnetic field of a magnet flows through the magnet and then radiates out from the end in all 360 degrees. To visualize this better, imagine holding a water hose. As the water rushes through the hose, it is fairly compact and compressed. When it hits the nozzle, it shoots out and up into the air in every direction like the cartoon to the right. Now imagine that as the water falls, it re-enters the hose from every direction and starts to head back up the hose again.

The question now is, How does this apply to what you observed during the experiment? You should have found that the magnet holds the most pins off the ends (or poles) and the fewest in middle. The reason for this is not known exactly except that the magnetic field spreads out from the ends of the magnet increasing the influence of the magnet at the end; whereas the middle of magnet compacts the magnetic field and reduces its ability to interact with the environment.

Science Fair Extensions

61. Add a second bar magnet to the first so that you have two magnets side by side, and see if the number of pins that you can attract changes in any of the areas that are tested.

62. Stack 10 to 12 donut magnets together, hold them like a roll of quarters and repeat the same experiment. You will find that this particular kind of magnet is magnetized as a long tube and then sliced like a loaf of bread producing a north and south pole on the faces of the donuts.

Double Magnet Maps

The Experiment

If you are cruising along through these labs in consecutive order, you have no doubt come to the conclusion that there is an invisible magnetic field surrounding every magnet. The next step in this adventure is to explore both ends of these magnets and figure out what makes them tick, and how they are similar and how they are different.

This particular lab draws on a device that you created out of a shoe box to study magnetic fields. If you have that magnetic field viewer handy, hooray! If not, we will give you instructions to create another one. Using this viewer, two magnets, and a pile of iron filings, we are going to create patterns that allow you to see magnetic fields when two magnets are placed together.

Materials

1	Shoe box lid
1	Bottle of iron filings
1	Pair of scissors
1	Sheet of plastic wrap
1	Roll of tape
2	Donut magnets
2	Cow magnets
2	Bar magnets
1	Pencil

Procedure

1. To make your magnetic field viewer, begin by cutting the center from the lid of the shoe box. Flip the shoe box lid upside down and place a square of plastic wrap on the inside of the lid and tape it in place. There is a cartoon illustration that will help on page 91. Flip the shoe box lid over and you are ready to go.

2. To create the first picture, place the two bar magnets under the shoe box lid with like poles facing each other, like the drawing on page 128. Center the magnets in the cellophane window. Once the magnets are centered, sprinkle iron filings all over the top of the shoe box lid. Be generous; you will be able to recycle them.

3. Once you have the filings on the lid, gently tap the edge of the box and the filings will align in the natural pattern of the lines of force. Draw a picture of the magnetic fields that are created when the like poles of two magnets are placed together.

4. When you have completed that drawing, reverse one of the bar magnets so that you now have two opposite poles, one north and the other south, facing each other. Sprinkle the iron filings on the magnetic field viewer again and create another pattern. Draw that pattern in the second box.

5. Repeat this procedure for the other two magnets. Draw the patterns that you see on separate sheets of paper.

Double Magnet Maps

Data & Observations

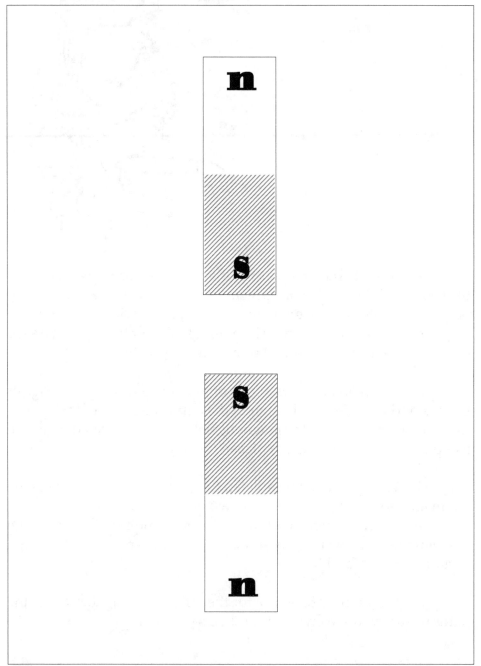

Opposites Attract • B. K. Hixson

Double Magnet Maps

How Come, Huh?

The iron filings you sprinkled on the shoe box lid each behave like miniature magnets, with a north and south pole. The magnetic fields of the two magnets influence the filings, and the filings move to reflect the lines of force coming from the fields.

Like poles repel, so when you placed the two bar magnets together with the north ends facing one another you should have produced a pattern that showed the magnetic lines of force working against one another, pushing away from the ends of the poles. We are guessing it may have looked something like the picture to the upper right.

Opposites poles, on the other hand, attract one another, so the second magnet map should have looked similar to the drawing to the lower right. The lines of force should have been flowing toward one another.

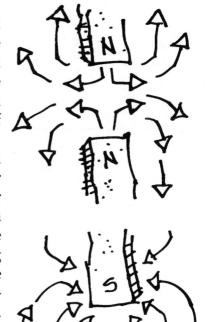

Science Fair Extensions

63. Figure out a way to determine the orientation of two pieces of lodestone, and use them to re-create the patterns that you made using the bar magnets.

64. Determine a way to use Ferrofluid to show the attraction and repulsion of magnetic poles.

65. Mix and match magnets, donut and bar, and so on.

Levitating Magnets

The Experiment

You can use two, like-magnetic fields to create the illusion of a magnet floating in midair. In fact, you can expand this idea and create a situation where it looks like several magnets are floating in midair with nothing but your good looks to hold them up. Magic? No, something even weirder and harder to explain—magnetic fields. Here's what you need to do.

Materials

5   Donut magnets
1   Pencil
1   Straw, plastic
1   Metric ruler

Procedure

1. Bring the two donut magnets together, flat side to flat side. One of two things will happen, either they will immediately be attracted to one another and stick, or they will repel one another and push apart. Mark the sides that repel with an X, using a pencil.

2. Once you have figured out which pole is which, slide one magnet onto the straw and let it glide all the way down to your fingers. Then place the second donut magnet on the straw so that the side that repels the first magnet slides down. Observe what happens. Measure the distance between the two magnets with the metric ruler and record that information in the Data & Observations section.

Levitating Magnets

3. Add a third donut magnet to the straw, check to make sure that the donut is going to repel off the second donut. Measure the distance and record that information in the chart below.

4. Repeat this procedure adding a fourth and fifth donut to the pig pile. Record the distances between magnets each time you add a new magnet. Use the illustration to the right as a guide to help you correctly identify the magnets.

Data & Observations

Record the distance between magnets, in millimeters, for each of the following conditions.

# Magnets	2	3	4	5
1 and 2				
2 and 3				
3 and 4				
4 and 5				

How Come, Huh?

Remember like poles repel, which is why the first two magnets pushed away from one another creating the space that you measured.

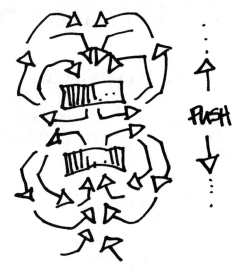

As you added magnets, the magnetic field between magnets one and two was compressed by the weight of the third magnet above. The more weight, the smaller the distance between the lower two magnets. Add a fourth magnet, and the distance is compressed even more. The same thing happens when you add a fifth magnet.

Science Fair Extensions

66. If you have a huge pile of donut magnets and a very long straw, you can set up an experiment designed to figure out if there is a point at which the magnetic field between magnets one and two gets so squished that it appears to be nonexistent.

67. Figure out a way to levitate book magnets. These are prepared the same way that the donut magnets are made—a long rectangle of material is magnetized and then sliced like a loaf of bread. The north and south poles are on the large faces.

68. Dig into the information on levitated trains. They are in use in Asia and Europe. They will soon be here in North America. Find out why they can travel up to 200 m.p.h.

What's the Buzz?

The Experiment

The final lab in this section is actually a fun demonstration of magnetic fields that you can show your friends, display in your room, and use to astonish your grandparents when they come over for the holidays. You are going to create a bee that hovers over a flower.

Materials

2   Donut magnets
6   Pipe cleaners
    1   yellow
    1   black
    2   white
    1   green
    1   red
2   Pieces of thread
1   Roll of masking tape
1   Shoe box

BODY OF BEE

Procedure

1. Holding the black and yellow pipe cleaners side by side, wrap them around one of the donut magnets to form the body of the bumblebee.

2. Make a loop in the shape of a wing and insert it inside the body of the bee. Use the illustration to the right as a guide. Do this twice, so that you have two wings.

WINGS

BEE

FLOWER

3. Wrap the red pipe cleaner around the disc magnet to make the center of the flower, and add green pipe cleaners to make the leaves. Use the illustration above as a guide.

4. Tie one piece of thread to each side of the bee, forming a triangle to use to hang the bee. Tie one end of the remaining string to the top of the triangle. Use the drawing to the right for help.

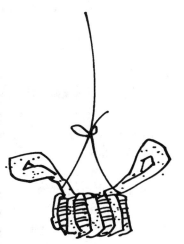

5. Place the flower in the empty shoe box. Punch a hole in the top of your box, so that you can hang the thread from the side of the box.

6. Slowly lower the thread until the magnetic field of the bee starts to come in contact with the magnetic field of the flower. If the bee is attracted to the flower, flip the flower over. If the bee hovers but is repelled by the flower, then you are in business. Tape the other end of the thread in place on the box.

7. If everything is working according to Hoyle, the bee will hover over the flower. Every now and then it gets stuck in one spot, but all you have to do is give it a little nudge, and it is off and flying again.

8. If you are feeling creative, you can add a background to the inside of the shoe box—a sun, some mountains, and trees. Perhaps you'll also add some other flowers and grass. Makes a snazzy Mother's Day present, and it could also be slipped into Santa's pack before he leaves for the North Pole.

What's the Buzz?

How Come, Huh?

This goes back to the levitating magnets lab—like poles repel. North poles repel north poles, and south poles repel south poles. In this case like poles were facing each other, causing the magnets to push away from, or repel, one another. The bee magnet would get pushed away, but gravity would shove it back over the flower magnet. The magnetic fields start to repel one another again, and the bee goes zinging off into space. Science and entertainment all in one package—what a country.

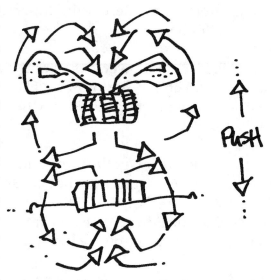

Science Fair Extensions

69. Repeat the experiment with book magnets and make flying fish, worms, snakes, or anything else that your imagination desires to bring to the world. Use the same concept, just a different shape for the magnet.

70. Use the idea of like poles repelling to create a cannon that shoots magnets into the air. Once you have figured out how you are going to do this, challenge one of your friends to a contest. Set up a target a reasonable distance away from the cannon and see who can shoot the most magnets into the target.

Big Idea 9

Magnets can also be created using electricity, and when electricity flows through a wire, it produces a detectable magnetic field.

Electric Magnetic Effect

The Experiment

Bring a compass near a piece of wire, and it will ignore the silly piece of metal. Run an electric current through the same piece of wire, and the compass will immediately take notice. Electron envy? Probably not, just another case of organizing charged particles so that they produce a magnetic field.

Materials

1   Ring stand
2   Rings
1   Roll of bare copper wire
1   Index card
1   Compass
1   Pencil
2   Alligator clips
1   Battery, 6 volt

Procedure

1. Using the ring stand or some other suitable apparatus, place one ring in the middle of the stand and the other near the top.

2. Cut a 12-inch piece of bare wire and loop one end around the *side* of the top ring, leaving about an inch-long tail at the top.

3. Punch a small hole in the center of the index card with the wire, and thread the bottom of the wire through the hole.

4. Drop the wire through the center of the middle ring. Balance the index card on the ring so that it is supported. Let the wire hang.

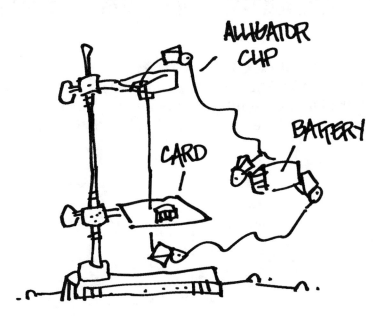

ALLIGATOR
CLIP

BATTERY

CARD

5. Using the compass as a guide, trace five circles around the hole in the index card. Note any movement of the needle as you bring it close to the wire.

6. Attach one alligator clip to the tail of wire at the top of the ring stand and the other alligator clip to the wire at the bottom of the stand. Place the compass on one of the circles on the index card. Note any needle movement—there should be none.

7. Connect both alligator clips to the terminals of the battery. Juice is now flowing through the wire. Observe what happens to the needle of the compass.

8. Move the compass from circle to circle noting whether the north pole or the south pole is pointing toward the wire. Record your observations for each compass location in the Data & Observations section found on the next page.

9. Finally, reverse the direction the electricity flows by switching the alligator clips on the battery terminals. By doing this the electricity flows the other way. Check all compass points again.

Electric Magnetic Effect

Data & Observations

1. Move the compass from circle to circle noting whether the north pole or the south pole is pointing toward the wire. Record your observations for each compass location in the circles below.

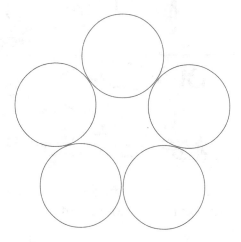

2. With the alligator clips *reversed*, note the position of the needle in each location.

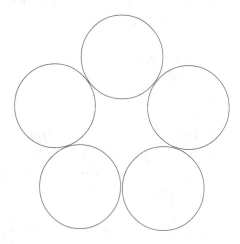

How Come, Huh?

Electrons are negatively charged particles. When they are stored in a battery, they leave the negative terminal and migrate through the circuit toward the positive terminal.

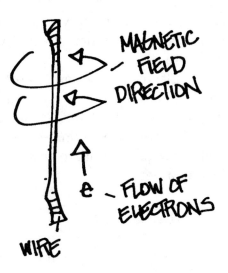

Since they are charged, they move in an orderly fashion, lined up, traveling in unison. When this happens, a weak magnetic field is produced around the wire. This weak magnetic field can be detected by the compass needle, which swings toward the wire. When the alligator leads are reversed, the electrons switch direction changing the magnetic field that is produced. With the electrons flowing the other way, the magnetic field is reversed. This is reflected in the compass readings that you took.

Science Fair Extensions

71. Experiment with the diameter of the copper wire and see if it has any affect on the size or influence of the magnetic field. Experiment with multiple strands of copper wire, twisted together to create a larger wire.

72. Try a piece of bell wire. This wire has a plastic coating surrounding the wire. Does the magnetic field pass through the plastic coating or is it an effective insulator? Experiment with other materials that may insulate the wire. Try masking tape, Styrofoam, plastic wrap, paper bags—let your imagination run wild.

Electrified Nail Coils

The Experiment

Take an ordinary nail, wrap it with several loops of copper wire, and hook a battery to it—you have an electromagnet, a magnet that was created when electricity flowed through a wire around an iron core.

Electromagnets and the other ideas that you are learning about are the foundation for all modern-day electric motors. A car starts and runs because it has an electromagnet in its motor. Most countertop kitchen appliances, home-repair tools, and other electrical devices that run with a motor are powered with an electromagnet. So without further adieu . . .

Materials

1   Coil of bell wire
1   Pair of wire strippers/cutters
1   16-Penny nail, ungalvanized
1   Box of paper clips, small
1   Battery holder
1   D Battery
2   Alligator clips
1   Compass
1   Bottle of iron filings
1   Sheet of paper

Procedure

1. Cut a 24-inch length of bell wire from the coil and strip both ends. To strip the end of a wire, you place about one-half inch of wire in the wire stripper, clamp down, and pull the wire through the little hole. The wire stripper should have cut through the plastic but not the metal; when you pulled, the plastic insulation should have come off, exposing the copper wire inside.

2. Leave a 4-inch tail and wrap one loop of wire around the nail as tightly as you can. Add a second loop right next to the first. Do this until you have a total of 10 loops on the nail. Use the illustration to the right as a guide.

Lower the nail into a pile of paper clips and see how many you can attract. Hopefully none—but in the spirit of establishing a control we had to try.

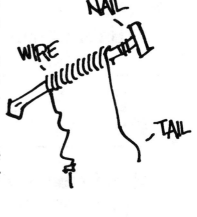

3. Snap the D battery into the battery holder and attach an alligator clip to each end of the battery holder.

4. Attach the loose end of each alligator clip to the bell wire that you stripped to complete the circuit. As soon as the circuit is completed, the electricity will start to flow through the wires wrapped around the nail and you will have created an electromagnet.

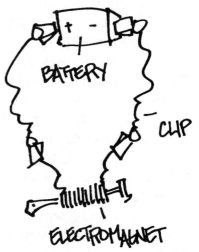

5. Dip the electromagnet into a pile of paper clips and see how many you can pick up with your newly constructed electromagnet. Count them and record this number in the data table on the next page in the square that correlates to 10 wraps and a 16-penny nail.

6. Continue to experiment by increasing the number of wraps around the nail in increments of 10. Record the number of paper clips that you pick up each time.

Electrified Nail Coils

Data & Observations

# Wraps	10	20	30	40	50
# Paper clips					

How Come, Huh?

We know that when electricity flows through a wire it produces a magnetic field around the wire. This is because electricity is made up of electrons that are zipping through the wire, like water moving through a hose. As the electrons flow through the wire, they are lined up in an orderly fashion producing a magnetic field that organizes the iron particles in the nail. Once the iron particles in the nail are lined up, this creates the magnetic field that we observe with the compass and the iron filings.

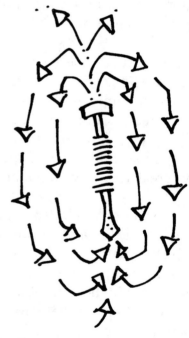

Science Fair Extensions

73. Experiment with different kinds of cores. The question being, "Are all electromagnets built with nails or can we use other objects?" Try a plastic straw, a wooden craft stick, a steel bolt, an aluminum can, and other ideas.

74. See if the strength of the battery has any influence on the strength of the electromagnet. Use a 6-volt lantern battery, a 9-volt transistor battery, and compare the number of pins you pick up.

75. Change the size of the core. Substitute a 12-penny nail and an 8-penny nail for the 16-penny nail. Compare the number of paper clips that you collect with every 10 wraps and see if there is a difference.

76. Create an electromagnet using very tight, neat, orderly wraps and another one that has the same number of wraps but that are placed around the core in a messy, disorderly fashion. Compare the ability of the two electromagnets to attract paper clips.

Mapping EM Fields

The Experiment

If you have not done the previous lab titled, Electrified Nail Coils, you need to plunk it in reverse and take about 20 minutes or so to get that lab under your belt.

Now, knowing that an iron core wrapped with copper wire produces a magnetic effect, we are going to stop and take a peek at what the magnetic field looks like.

Materials

1   16-Penny nail, ungalvanized
1   Box of paper clips, small
1   Coil of bell wire
1   Pair of wire strippers
1   Battery holder
1   D Battery
2   Alligator clips
1   Compass
1   Bottle of iron filings
1   Sheet of paper

Procedure

Using the directions found on pages 142–143, wrap an electromagnet with 50 coils.

Data & Observations

1. Now that you have created a working electromagnet, it is time to check to see what kind of magnetic field it produces. Trace the outline of the electromagnet inside the box on the next page. Using the compass, trace outlines of the compass around the nail, recording the position of the needle in each place. Using this information, figure out the pattern and shape of the magnetic field.

Mapping EM Fields

2. Copy this page. Place the electromagnet *under* the rectangle on the copy. With the juice flowing through the wires, sprinkle the iron filings on the copy. Tap the edge of the sheet to line up the filings. Draw a picture of the pattern that you see and compare it with the pattern that you created using the compass.

How Come, Huh?

The minute you hook the coil of wire around the nail to a source of electricity, the current starts to flow. As the electricity flows through the wire, it produces a weak magnetic field—as evidenced in the first lab of this section. This magnetic field passes into the nail and comes in contact with the iron particles.

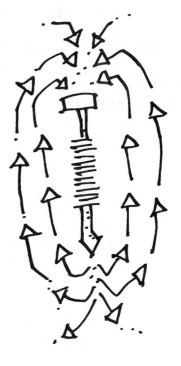

The magnetic field does not just have a passing, casual interest in the iron filings. It grabs ahold of each atom and starts to line them up in a precise and consistent order—just like a drill sergeant in the army. As these atoms are lined up, they also start to produce a magnetic field that is then detected by both the compass and the iron filings that you sprinkled on the paper.

When the electricity is disconnected from the electromagnet, some of the residual effect is maintained, but over time the iron particles, which are in constant motion, tend to discombobulate themselves and wind up in a random pattern that does not produce a detectable magnetic field.

Science Fair Extensions

77. Change the shape of the iron core. Find an iron ring and see what the magnetic field looks like. Try a piece of metal that has been bent into a large *S* shape. What happens when you use a piece of iron that is at right angles?

78. Design an experiment that allows you to use Ferrofluid to detect the presence of a magnetic field.

Flipping Poles

The Experiment

This lab is not an offshoot of some obscure logging competition from the high Cascades of British Columbia, but rather a look at what happens when you switch the direction that the electrons inside the wire are moving. We had a sample of this idea in the lab Electric Magnetic Effect, and we are going to follow up on it.

If you have not done the lab titled, Electrified Nail Coils. You need to shift gears and take about 20 minutes or so to build an understanding of electromagnets and how they are constructed.

Materials

1   16-Penny nail, ungalvanized
1   Coil of bell wire
1   Pair of wire strippers
1   Battery holder
1   D Battery
2   Alligator clips
2   Compasses

Procedure

1. Using the directions found on pages 142–143, wrap an electromagnet with 50 coils.

2. Trace the outline of the electromagnet in the box on the next page. Place the compasses on either end of the electromagnet. Draw the position of the needles at the end of the electromagnet.

3. Now reverse the wires on the battery clip, put the electromagnet in the exact same position and show the position of the needle. Describe any differences or similarities with the first experiment in the space provided on the next page.

Data & Observations

1. Place the electromagnet in the box and draw the position of the compass needles at either end.

2. Reverse the position of the alligator clips on the battery and draw a picture of the position of the compass needles again.

How Come, Huh?

Electrons are negatively charged particles. When they are summoned from their resting place in a battery, they leave via the negative terminal and migrate through the circuit to the other terminal.

When you reverse the alligator clips, you reverse the direction the electricity is flowing through the wire. When this happens, you also cause the magnetic field to flip-flop and change. Using the compasses makes this easier to see.

Science Fair Extensions

79. Does the size of the electromagnet affect the outcome of this lab?

Wire Wars

The Experiment

With magnetic fields flying all around the place, it's hard to imagine that there is not a lot of conflict, particularly between parallel wires. This is something that you are going to prove.

Materials

1 Wire coat hanger
1 Roll of masking tape
1 Sheet of aluminum foil
1 Pair of scissors
2 Alligator clips
1 6-Volt battery

Procedure

1. Using the illustration to the upper right as a guide, bend the wire coat hanger into the shape shown. Make several wraps of masking tape over the hanger to insulate it.

2. Cut a strip of aluminum foil a half an inch wide and about 20 inches long. Tape this strip on the hanger as shown above.

3. Attach two alligator clips to the terminals on the battery. Touch the other end of each alligator clip to the top of each end of the foil, as shown to the right. Observe what happens

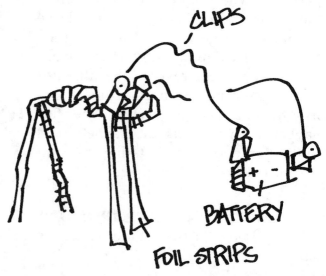

Opposites Attract • B. K. Hixson

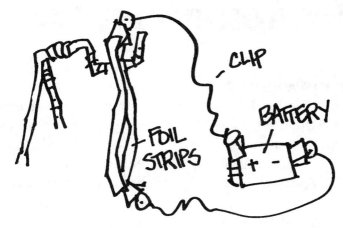

4. Now twist the top two leads of the aluminum foil together and clip one alligator clip on the top. Gently touch the other alligator clip to the very bottom of the loop. Observe what happens. Use the illustration above as a guide to help you.

Data & Observations

Circle the word that best describes what happened when you attached the leads from the battery to the wire.

1. Both leads at the top caused the wire to be . . .

   ATTRACTED   REPELLED

2. One lead at the top and the other at the bottom caused the wire to be . . .

   ATTRACTED   REPELLED

How Come, Huh?

When you apply an electric current to a wire, it creates a magnetic field that circles the wire. See the Electric Magnetic Effect lab. If you have two wires side by side each producing their own magnetic field, they are going to repel one another—the fancy way to say bump into and push one another away—if the current is flowing in opposite directions. If it is flowing in the same direction, they will attract one another.

Science Fair Extensions

80. Vary the strength of the battery for different results.

Galvanometers, Etc.

The Experiment

Hook a wire up to a battery full of electrons, and the electrons instantly zip into the wire. Not only do they deliver energy to the desired destination, but a magnetic field is also produced along the entire length of the wire. An electric current in a wire produces a magnetic field. You knew that. How about the reverse of that situation?

This lab will allow you to build an instrument called a galvanometer that will allow you to demonstrate that a magnetic field can also produce an electric current in a wire. The exact opposite of what you have been seeing? Why not.

Materials

1   Piece of cardboard, 3" by 4"
1   Roll of insulated bell wire
1   Pair of wire strippers
1   D Battery
1   D Battery clip
2   Alligator clips
1   Compass
1   Bar magnet

Procedure

1. Using the pattern on the next page, fold one-inch supports on each side of the cardboard.

2. Leave a 6-inch tail and wrap 30 wraps of wire around the middle of the galvanometer. Leave another 6-inch tail and cut the wire from the roll.

3. Using the wire strippers, remove a half an inch of insulation off each tail, leaving nothing but bare wire exposed.

4. Snap the battery into the battery clip, and add an alligator clip to each side.

5. Slide the compass inside and under the wire that is around the piece of cardboard and see if the compass deflects (moves) at all. Rotate the compass and observe the position of the needle as you rotate it under the wire.

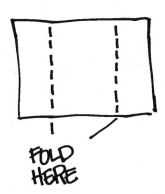

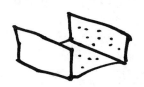

FOLD HERE

6. Rotate the piece of cardboard so that the compass needle is perpendicular to the loop of wire. See the illustration on the next page as a guide.

7. Hook one alligator clip up to each stripped end of the wire wrapped around the cardboard. Observe the position of the compass needle.

8. Congratulations! You have just built an instrument called a galvanometer. It is used by scientists to detect weak electric currents. But hang in there, you are only halfway through this lab. Now you are going to prove that a magnetic field can produce a weak electric current in a wire.

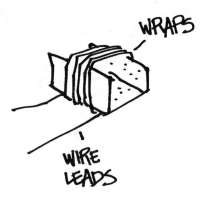

WRAPS

WIRE LEADS

Galvanometers, Etc.

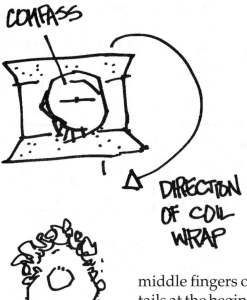

COMPASS

DIRECTION OF COIL WRAP

9. Disconnect the two alligator clips. The compass needle should have returned to its original position, which lets you know that a magnetic field is no longer present because an electric current is no longer flowing through the wire.

10. You are going to make another coil of wire. This time loosely wrap the wire around the three middle fingers of your left hand. Leave 6-inch tails at the beginning and end, just like you did with the galvanometer.

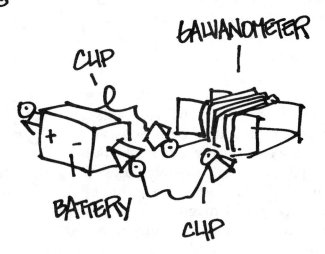

GALVANOMETER

CLIP

BATTERY

CLIP

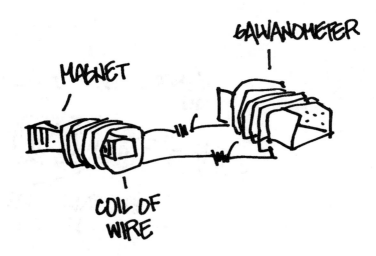

MAGNET

GALVANOMETER

COIL OF
WIRE

11. Strip the ends of the wire and twist and connect the ends of the coil with the ends of the loop. This forms a giant circuit. Use the illustration at the top of the page as a guide.

12. Holding the loop in one hand and the magnet in the other, move the magnet in and out of the loop quickly. As you do, observe what happens to the compass needle.

How Come, Huh?

1. Following instruction 5, you placed the compass under the wire loop in the cardboard support. As you rotated the compass, the needle should have also rotated to always point to magnetic north. No current in the wire, no magnetic field, nothing to attract the needle in the compass. Three and out.

2. When you hooked the juice up to the wire loop, a magnetic field was produced. The way you know this is that the compass needle aligned with the wire loop. The only reason this would happen is if a magnetic field suddenly appeared to wrangle the needle into position.

In summary, you hook the wire loop to a battery, the electricity starts to flow, the electrons flowing through the wire produce a weak magnetic field that attracts the compass needle. Unhook the battery and the compass needle rotates back to its original position.

Galvanometers, Etc.

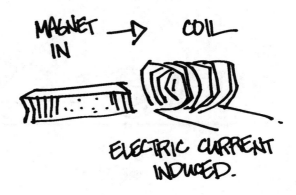

MAGNET IN → COIL

ELECTRIC CURRENT INDUCED.

3. When you inserted the magnet in the coil loop, the magnetic field of that magnet induced, or started, the electrons in the wire to flow. The moving electrons are defined as a current, and an electric current flowing through a wire produces a magnetic field. The magnetic field in the wire attracted the compass needle, and you now have proof positive that a magnet can create a weak electric current. You are also a blossoming expert on galvanometer construction.

Science Fair Extensions

81. Design an experiment that allows you to test the effect of increasing or decreasing the number of loops in the coil on the strength of the magnetic field.

82. Double up the bar magnet you use or substitute a stronger magnet, like a cow magnet, and determine how that affects the outcome of your experiment.

83. Use your galvanometer to demonstrate that the magnetic field in a coil of wire is reversed when the leads connecting the coil to the battery are reversed. In other words, substitute the galvanometer for the electromagnet in the experiment titled Flipping Poles.

Opposites Attract • B. K. Hixson

Loop Interrupted

The Experiment

From the previous lab you have intimate and current knowledge that a magnet inserted into a coil of wire produces a weak electric current in that wire. What if the coil or loop is not closed? Same effect or different? Time to lab.

Materials

2   Wire coat hangers
2   8-Inch lengths of 12-gauge copper wire
1   Bar magnet
1   Roll of cotton string
1   Pair of scissors
1   Soldering iron
1   Roll of solder
    Adult Supervision

Procedure

1. Using the illustration below as a guide, construct a stand to support each of the loops that you will make.

2. Using the 12-gauge (or heavier) copper wires, form two loops—one that you solder closed with the assistance of an adult, and the other you leave open, leaving a gap of about one-half inch.

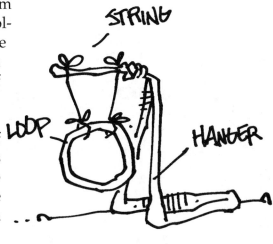

3. Cut four pieces of cotton string, each 6 inches long, and tie two to the top half of each loop. Use the illustration to the right as a guide.

Loop Interrupted

4. You should now have two loops—one open, one closed, each hanging from its own stand. Take the bar magnet and move it in and out of the open loop. Observe what happens—if anything—to the loop. Note any movement.

5. Repeat the procedure for the closed loop, moving it in and out of the loop rapidly. Observe what happens—if anything—to the loop. Note any movement.

Data & Observations

Circle the word that best describes what happened when you inserted the magnet in the loop.

1. When you moved the magnet in and out of an open loop, it:

   MOVED   DID NOT MOVE

2. When you moved the magnet in and out of a closed loop, it:

   MOVED   DID NOT MOVE

How Come, Huh?

When you inserted the bar magnet in the closed loop, it induced, or started, an electrical current moving around the loop. You know that when a current is moving through the wire it causes a magnetic field to be created. The magnetic field of the loop and the magnetic field of the magnet attract and repel one another causing the loop to swing back and forth.

When you repeated the experiment using the open loop, no magnetic field was created because you have to have a complete circuit in order for the electrons to flow freely. When the magnet was

inserted in the loop, the electrons started to flow, but when they got to the gap, it was impossible for them to cross. Kind of like taking a trip from Arizona to Utah and coming upon the Grand Canyon—kind of kills your incentive to keep driving straight ahead without your handy Buck Rogers jet pack.

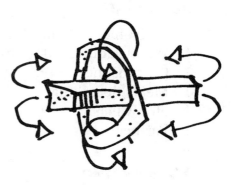

Science Fair Extensions

84. Design an experiment that allows you to determine if and how the thickness of the wire affects the amount of current that is induced, or started, and the strength of the magnetic field that is created.

85. Experiment with the strength of the magnet that is inserted into the loop. Determine if the type of magnet has any effect on the amount of movement.

Eddy Currents

The Experiment

One final idea before we leave this section. We have been cramming magnets under boards, through loops, into coils, and at each other. In this last experiment we are going to introduce the idea of eddy currents.

An eddy current is created when a strong magnet drops through a metallic (but not iron) tube. The effect, as you will see, is much different than if you were to drop a nonmagnetic object through the same tube.

Materials

1   PVC pipe, 1" diam., 3" long
1   Wooden dowel, 0.75" by 3"
1   Cow magnet
1   Metal pipe, 1" diam., 3" long
1   Stopwatch
1   Partner

Procedure

1. Hold the PVC pipe straight up and down, like the illustration to the right, and drop the wooden dowel through the tube. Ask your partner to record the amount of time that it takes for the dowel to travel the full length of the tube. Enter that number in the Data & Observations section to the right. Repeat the test three more times and then determine the average time.

2. Repeat the experiment using the cow magnet. Record these times in the data table.

3. Repeat the experiments again, this time using a metal, but not iron, tube. Drop the cow magnet and the wood dowel through each tube three times and average the data you collect.

Data & Observations

Tube	PVC			Metal		
Object/Trial	1	2	3	4	5	6
Dowel						
Cow Magnet						

How Come, Huh?

When you drop the magnet into the metal tube, the magnetic field surrounding it constantly changes as it falls. This changing field induces, or starts, the flow of eddy currents in an electrical conductor. These eddy currents produce a magnetic field that repels, or pushes, against the falling magnet, causing it to slow down.

Science Fair Extensions

86. Experiment with different kinds of metal tubes. See if you can rank the different kinds of metals in order of their ability to produce eddy currents and resist the movement of the magnets.

87. Try magnets of differing strengths and see if this affects the size and strength of the eddy currents that are produced. The stronger the currents, the slower the magnets will fall.

88. Determine if the length of the tube has any effect on the speed the magnet falls or the amount of time that it takes for the magnet to emerge from the pipe's end.

Big Idea 10

Magnets can be used for technology, ogy, medicine, transportation, research, and entertainment.

Opposites Attract • B. K. Hixson

BB Races

The Experiment

Over the years there have been lots of different kinds of games that have incorporated magnetism. In particular there was a game you could buy at toy stores that featured a small plastic bee with a magnetic tail insert. The bee was trapped between two pieces of plastic. The object of the game was to use a magnetic wand to move the bee through a maze from flower to flower without falling into a variety of hazards, represented by holes in the board.

This activity is an adaptation of that age-old idea. You are going to create a maze of your design. An iron bb is going to be placed at the starting point of the maze, and you will compete against your colleagues to see who can get through the maze in the least amount of time, avoiding as many obstacles as possible.

Materials

3   Sheets of plain, white paper
1   Black marker
1   Sheet of corrugated cardboard, 8.5" by 11"
1   Utility knife
1   Bottle of glue or glue gun
1   Sheet of tagboard, 8.5" by 11"
1   Sheet of clear acetate, 8.5" by 11"
6   Large, thick books
1   Iron bb
1   Strong magnet
1   Watch with a second hand

Procedure

1. This is where you get to let your imagination run wild. Draw a maze on a sheet of plain paper. The width of the maze track should be about a half an inch. Your objective is to create a maze that travels from one end of the cardboard to another. Be sure to include dead ends, hazards, and potholes. A sample of a section of the maze is provided on page 166. Yours will be much larger and more extensive.

BB Races

2. When you get the maze to the point that you are happy with it, copy it onto the piece of corrugated cardboard. Then, with the help of an adult, cut out the track of the maze. You can make indentations in the cardboard that serve as hazards.

3. Glue the maze down onto the tagboard, and then glue the acetate cover on top of the maze. Your maze now has a bottom and a top. The only way in and out of the maze is through the starting and ending slots that you have created.

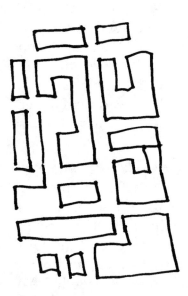

Data & Observations

To play the game you support the maze on a pile of books, 3 on each end. Use the picture above as a guide. Place the bb at the start of the maze. After looking at the watch, the timer says "Go!" and the person who is competing places the magnet under the cardboard and propels the bb through the maze as fast as he or she can. If you fall into a hazard, you get a 5-second penalty. The object of the game is to move through the maze as quickly as possible. The winner is the person who has the fastest time after the hazard penalties have been added in.

How Come, Huh?

The iron in the bb is attracted to the magnet. Since magnetic fields can penetrate objects like cardboard, they attract the bb through the cardboard and allow you to guide it along the maze.

Science Fair Extensions

89. Take a large piece of cardboard and, instead of a maze, make a freeway. Build cars around flat, book magnets, and go driving on your freeway using magnets to drive the cars from underneath.

90. Design a three-dimensional, cardboard bb park, like a skateboard park. Include ramps, half pipes, waves, and other obstacles, and run your competition the same way that you did with the maze.

Fi Ling's Hair Club

The Experiment

There are a number of games out on the market that take advantage of the fact that iron filings, trapped between two thin sheets of plastic can be moved and placed to create pictures. We are going to take a minute, have a little fun with this, and give Mr. Ling, Fi to his friends, a new, magnetically inspired hairdo.

Materials

1   Petri dish
1   Sheet of paper
1   Pen, pencil, or marker
1   Cow magnet
1   Pair of scissors
1   Bottle of iron filings

Procedure

1. Remove the top from the petri dish. Take the bottom of the petri dish and trace the outline of the smaller of the two halves onto a sheet of paper.

2. Once you have the disk cut out, you will want to copy a picture of Fi Ling on your circle of paper. You can find a picture of his face on the opposite page.

3. Place your drawing of Fi Ling inside the larger of the two halves of the petri dishes. Sprinkle several iron filings on top of his face and place the smaller—top half—of the petri dish upside down, inside the larger half of the petri dish.

4. Placing the cow magnet under the dish, drag the iron filings around, herding them into the locations that you would like them stay. You can give Fi Ling hair, a full beard, a fu manchu, sideburns; you name it—have fun.

Data & Observations

Draw two different versions of Fi Ling that you created using the faces in the circles pictured below.

How Come, Huh?

Iron filings are attracted to the magnet. When you move the magnet, some of the iron filings follow until you lift the magnet off the plastic and the filings fall into place. If the filings were not made of iron or if your magnet lost its organization, this experiment would not work.

Science Fair Extensions

91. Draw a Chihuahua and put hair on him too. In fact you could draw just about anything and do the same thing that we are doing here.

The Motor Effect

The Experiment

We are building up to the big finale for this book, a couple of simple, portable, electric motors. A motor is essentially a large coil of wire that spins in response to the presence of a magnetic field. This is what happens every time you jump in the car and turn over the ignition, start the blender, fire up the lawn mower, or use any other machine that incorporates a motor.

To better under-stand what causes the ini-tial movement that gets these motors going, you are going to explore what is called the motor effect using a couple of magnets and a simple electrified wire.

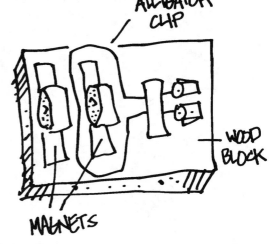

Materials

4 Donut magnets
1 Roll of masking tape
1 Wood board, 1" by 4" by 6"
3 Alligator clips
1 D Battery
1 D Battery clip

Procedure

1. Insert the battery into the battery clip and attach one alligator lead to each terminal.

2. Stack the four donut magnets into a pile and then divide them into two groups of two. Tape the magnets to the board, using the illustration to the upper right as a guide—north pole facing south pole leaving a gap of about one-half inch.

3. Tape the third alligator clip in the position shown in the illustration on page 170. The wire should be between the two sets of magnets. Tape the alligator clips to the board as shown.

4. Connect one of the leads from the battery to the alligator clip that is closest. Touch the other set of alligator clips to one another and observe what happens to the wire. Reverse the leads and see if the direction that the wire moves is different or remains the same.

How Come, Huh?

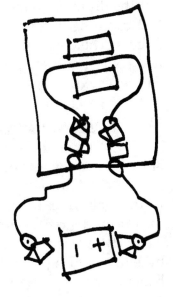

The four magnets produce a permanent magnetic field—just like the one that you created when you placed the two opposite poles facing one another in the lab, Double Magnet Maps, on page 126. When you connected the battery to the wire that was between the magnets, a second magnetic field surrounding the wire was produced. This magnetic field is going to be attracted to either the north pole (up) or the south pole (down) and will move in that direction. When you reverse the direction of the current in the wire, the magnetic field around the wire will also be reversed.

The Motor Effect

This all leads into one of the basic ideas of electricity that allows you to predict the direction of movement called the Right-Hand Rule.

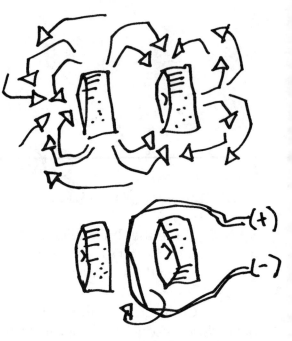

To use this rule you need to know two things, 1) the direction that the electricity is flowing (it leaves the battery at the negative terminal and re-enters the battery at the positive terminal), and 2) the orientation of the magnets (which can be determined using a compass).

Once you have determined the direction that the current is flowing, take your right hand and place it under the wire with your thumb sticking up. The wire should trace the position of your thumb like the drawing to the above right. Curl your fingers, forming a C. You can now predict the movement of the wire by looking at your fingers. The wire will either move up or down to mirror the direction that your fingers are pointing—another mystery of nature unraveled and revealed.

Science Fair Extensions

92. Change the diameter of the wire and see if the thickness has any affect on the rate or degree of movement.

93. Add or subtract magnets from the permanent magnetic field. Again, does the strength of the magnetic field affect, in any way, the rate or degree of movement in the wire.

94. Change the amount of electricity flowing through the wire by either adding batteries in series, increasing the voltage of the battery, or using a transformer with variable voltage.

A Simple Motor

The Experiment

We are definitely heading into the homestretch. Everything that you have been studying—all of the ideas that you have been poking and prodding—lead to your understanding of this one, big, idea: how a simple electric motor works.

We are going to use permanent magnets to create the magnetic field, a coil of wire to form the actual motor, and a felt marker will stand in for a decent commutator. Once you build this version we will turn you loose on the model that I built over and over as a fifth grader in Mr. Goffard's class—but, first things, first.

Materials

- 4 Donut magnets
- 2 Alligator leads
- 1 12-oz. Plastic cup
- 1 Roll of masking tape
- 2 Paper clips, large
- 1 Black, felt marker, permanent
- 1 Pair of wire strippers
- 1 2-Foot length of bell wire
- 1 D Battery
- 1 D Battery holder

Procedure

1. Insert the battery into the battery holder and attach one alligator lead to each terminal.

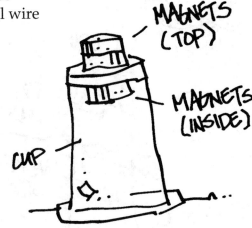

2. Make a stack out of the four donut magnets. Divide the stack in half and place two magnets inside the bottom of the cup and two additional magnets outside the bottom of the cup.

A Simple Motor

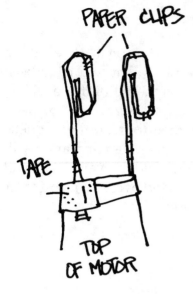

PAPER CLIPS

TAPE

TOP
OF MOTOR

3. Open the paper clips up and tape the extended portion of the paper clip to the bottom of the cup on either side of the magnets. Use the illustration to the left as a guide.

4. Leave a 2-inch tail and start to wrap a coil around two fingers on your hand. Wrap until all of the wire is used up, leaving another 2-inch tail.

Use the tails to make a single wrap around the coil and hold it in place. Adjust the tails so that they are sticking straight out. Strip two-thirds of the plastic off each tail.

BLACKEN

5. Using a permanent marker, blacken the top half of each tail. Be sure to blacken the same side on both tails.

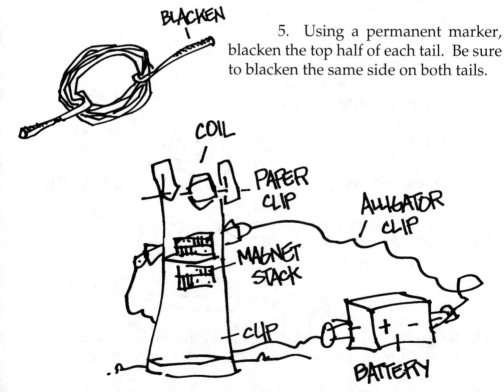

COIL

PAPER
CLIP

ALLIGATOR
CLIP

MAGNET
STACK

CUP

BATTERY

6. Slide the coil of wire into the supports. Use the illustration to the bottom left to help you.

7. Clip the alligator leads from the battery to the base of each paper clip. When you connect the second lead, you will notice that the coil did one of three things, 1) started spinning, in which case you do nothing but holler, "Yahoo!" and shove your fist in the air, 2) wobbled, in which case give the coil a gentle twirl and it should start to spin, or 3) did nothing and you are going to have to troubleshoot. See below.

Troubleshooting

If you motor does not spin, try these things in this order.

1. Check your battery and make sure that it has juice.

2. Make sure that the alligator clips are connected to the metal tabs in the battery holder and not to a piece of the plastic.

3. Double-check the connection between the clip and the insulated wire; check for breaks in the alligator wire.

4. Straighten the tails coming from the coil. The coil should spin smoothly and without much wobbling when you spin it with your finger. If it does not , flatten the coil a bit and straighten the wire.

5. Check the position of the paper clips. They should be even. If one is higher than the other, the coil will be lopsided and have to work harder to spin. Make sure they are level.

6. Add a second battery for more juice or substitute either a lantern battery, 6-volt, or a variable, low-volt, power supply. By now your motor should be spinning. We have built thousands of these things and one of the reasons that we selected this design is because it is so kid-and adult-friendly—virtually any electrical nincompoop can build one.

A Simple Motor

After your motor spins for a while, you may notice that it starts working less efficiently. This is usually because the marker gets a little smeared. Clean the wire with a paper towel and re-mark the wire. Another common problem is that kids build these things, run them for hours, then they start to fritz. They readjust everything and still no spin. Get a new, fresh battery and this will solve your problem 99 percent of the time.

How Come, Huh?

The four magnets formed a permanent magnetic field. When you hooked the coil of wire to the battery, a magnetic field was produced around the coil. When these two magnetic fields come into close contact, there is movement. (If you just got here from The Motor Effect lab, this should sound very familiar.) The coil starts to move, but only temporarily.

It is temporary because you blackened the top half of each tail. This black ink served as an insulator so that when the coil makes half a spin, the electricity stops, the magnetic field disappears, but the coil continues to spin because it has momentum. When it completes its cycle, it comes in contact with the bare wire again, juice flows, magnetic fields are created, and the coil gets another push. Think of a bike that has been flipped upside down. You whack the wheel and it spins, you whack it again and it spins faster, you keep whacking the wheel each time it comes around and you have a lot of motion—same idea here.

Science Fair Extensions

95. Prove that the amount of electricity is directly proportional to the speed that the motor will spin.

96. Figure out other ways to insulate the top half of the wires that form the coil supports. Or, read up on commutators and figure out how to add one to your motor.

97. Experiment without insulating the coil supports.

Mr. Goffard's Motor

The Experiment

If you made it all the way to the end of the book and did not realize that it was dedicated to my fifth-grade teacher, Ed Goffard, that probably answers your first question, "Who the #&!!@ is Mr. Goffard?"

Among all of the other great science labs that we worked on that year, my all-time favorite was the motor that we are about to present to you. As I think back on it, it was my favorite because it was entirely our own. We did not use a kit or even a pattern. In fact, when I wanted to add it to this book, I called Mr. Goffard and reintroduced myself. After we got through all of the what-have-you-been-doings? and where-are-you-nows?, I explained what I was up to and asked if it would be possible to get a copy of the pattern. He replied that it would, after he sat down and thought it through for a bit. A couple of days later a hand-drawn replica of the motor that we built and rebuilt arrived in the mail. It is a throwback to the days when you went out into the garage and ripped apart the toaster, bicycle pump, and your old red wagon to make a spaceship—primeval cutting-edge science, if such an oxymoron exists.

We included it in the book not only because it is a very appropriate ending for a book on magnets, but also because there is so much that you can do to adapt the experiment. We are recommending a 6-volt lantern battery to you, but Mr. Goffard provided us with a variable resistance train transformer. What this meant was that if we built everything just right and assembled it perfectly, we could get the motor not only to run at an optimum and very entertaining speed, but we could also get it to produce a thunderous vibration and dance off the table. If you are thinking about reading ahead to find out how to do that, sorry, you'll have to figure that out on your own, just like we did 35 years ago.

Mr. Goffard's Motor

Materials

1	# 303 Soup can
1	Pair of tin snips
1	Hammer
4	8-Penny nails, ungalvanized
1	Piece of wood, 0.5" by 4" by 6"
2	Thumbtacks
1	Toilet-plunger shaft, brass
1	Roll of masking tape
1	Roll of magnet wire, enameled, 22 gauge
1	Piece of sandpaper, 80 grit
2	Brass washers, diam. of toilet shaft
2	Paper clips
1	2-Inch carriage bolt with 2 nuts,
2	0.5" Wood screws
1	Screwdriver
2	Alligator clips
1	6-Volt lantern battery

Procedure

1. The first thing that you want to do is make and assemble the armature supports. Remove both ends from the #303 soup can. Using the wire cutters, cut two strips from the can, 1 inch wide by 4 inches long. Flatten the metal strips using the hammer.

Take one of the 8-penny nails and make a hole one-half inch from each end of the strip. When you are done, it should look like the illustration to the right.

SUPPORT

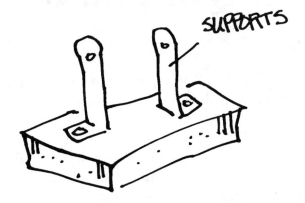

2. Bend the end of each support one inch from the end. Place the supports on the wood board and hold them in place using two of the thumbtacks. The supports should be 4 inches apart. Use the illustration above as a guide.

3. Next is the armature, or the spinning part of the motor. Cut the toilet-tank plunger with the tin snips so that it is 6 inches long. Hold the four nails, two pointing one direction and two pointing the other direction and tape them in place using the illustration below as a guide. Wrap the shaft with tape to insulate it also.

4. Once the nails and shaft are taped in place, start with a lead wire running down the shaft toward the nails. When you get to the nails, make very *tight* wraps from the center of the nails to the heads and back to the center. **VERY IMPORTANT**. When you cross over the shaft and start to wrap toward the nails on the other side of the shaft, DO NOT CHANGE THE DIRECTION YOU ARE WRAP-PING. Wrap from the center, down to the nail heads and back. Use the illustration to the right as a guide.

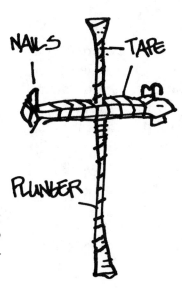

Mr. Goffard's Motor

5. To finish off your armature wrap run the wire back down the toilet-plunger shaft, on the opposite side, and tape the two wires in place.

6. Using the sandpaper, remove the enamel from the two center wires. This is also very important because magnet wire is coated with an enamel that prevents electron movement. If you do not scrape that off, the circuit will not be complete.

7. Slide the armature into the two supports. Use the picture below as a guide.

8. Once the armature is in place, slide the two brass washers on each end. Move them right up to the soup can supports and put a piece of tape on each end to keep them from sliding around.

9. Open the paper clip up. Place the opened paper clip near the shaft of the armature so that it comes in contact with the wires as pictured.

10. Secure the paper clip to the wood board with a thumbtack. Open the second paper clip and attach it so that it is making contact with the other side of the armature.

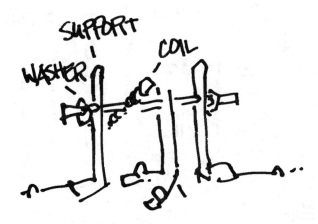

11. The last thing that you are going to want to do is make the electromagnet. Screw both nuts onto the ends of the bolt.

12. Leave a 4-inch tail of magnet wire and start wrapping wire from one side of the bolt to the other.

Make 4 complete layers of wraps, all going the same direction and leave a 4-inch tail after the last set of wraps. Your electromagnet is complete.

13. Place the electromagnet underneath the armature parallel to the shaft. Use the illustration on page 182 as a guide.

14. Attach one tail of the electromagnet to the paper clip (labeled contact) under the armature. Attach the other tail from the electromagnet to an alligator clip. Attach the second alligator clip to the other paper clip (labeled contact).

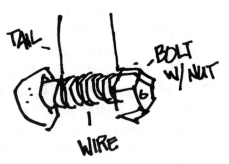

Mr. Goffard's Motor

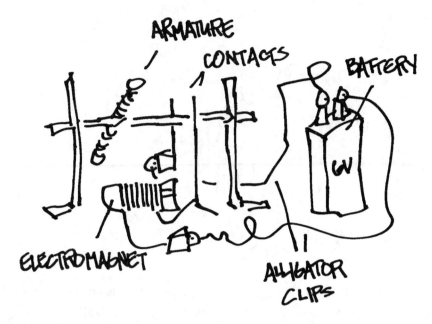

ARMATURE

CONTACTS

BATTERY

ELECTROMAGNET

ALLIGATOR CLIPS

15. To fire up your motor attach both alligator clips to the positive and negative terminals of the lantern battery. If the armature wiggles but won't spin, give it a little shove and it should be off and running.

How Come, Huh?

The electromagnet created a magnetic field when everything was hooked to the lantern battery. When you hooked the armature to the battery, a magnetic field was produced around that as well. When these two magnetic fields come into close contact, there is movement. (Remember The Motor Effect lab?) The coil starts to move, but only temporarily.

It is temporary because as soon as the shaft starts to spin, the wires lose contact with the paper clips, which means no juice. The electricity stops, the magnetic field disappears, but the coil continues to spin because it has momentum. When it completes its cycle, it comes in contact with the bare wire again, juice flows, magnetic fields are created, and the armature gets another push, just like the coil of wire in the simpler magnet in the previous lab. Think of a bike that has been flipped upside down. As the motor spins, loses contact with the wire, spins, loses contact with the wire, spins, and loses contact with the wire, it builds momentum due to the wire of the nails and the wrapped wires. A simpler name for all of this is a motor.

Science Fair Extensions

98. Exchange the two alligator clips, positive for negative, and decide how that affects the direction that your motor spins.

99. Build electromagnets of varying sizes (increasing or decreasing the number of wraps) and see if that has any effect on how well your motor spins.

100. Experiment with changing the direction of the wrap on the armature. See if it really does have an effect on the ability of the motor to spin or if we are full of it.

101. Substitute a train transformer for the lantern battery and see if you can get your motor to dance and vibrate across the table. Be sure to have adult supervision, we'd hate to have them miss the show.

Science Fair Projects
•
A Step-by-Step Guide: From Idea To Presentation

Opposites Attract • B. K. Hixson

Science Fair Projects

Ah, the impending science fair project—a good science fair project has the following five characteristics:

1. The student must come up with an *original* question.
2. That *original* question must be suited to an experiment in order to provide an answer.
3. The *original* idea is outlined with just one variable isolated.
4. The *original* experiment is performed and documented using the scientific method.
5. A presentation of the *original* idea in the form of a lab write-up and display board is completed.

Science Fair Projects

As simple as science fair versus science project sounds, it gets screwed up millions of times a year by sweet, unsuspecting students who are counseled by sweet, unknowing, and probably just as confused parents.

To give you a sense of contrast we have provided a list of legitimate science fair projects and then reports that do not qualify. We will also add some comments in italics that should help clarify why they do or do not qualify in the science fair project department.

Science Fair Projects

1. Temperature and the amount of time it takes mealworms to change to beetles.

Great start. We have chosen a single variable that is easy to measure: temperature. From this point forward the student can read, explore, and formulate an original question that is the foundation for the project.

A colleague of mine actually did a similar type of experiment for his master's degree. His topic: The rate of development of fly larva in cow poop as a function of temperature. No kidding. He found out that the warmer the temperature of the poop the faster the larva developed into flies.

2. The effect of different concentrations of soapy water on seed germination.

Again, wonderful. Measuring the concentration of soapy water. This leads naturally into original questions and a good project.

3. Crystal size and the amount of sugar in the solution.

This could lead into other factors such as exploring the temperature of the solution, the size of the solution container, and other variables that may affect crystal growth. Opens a lot of doors.

vs. Science Reports

4. Helicopter rotor size and the speed at which it falls.

Size also means surface area, which is very easy to measure. The student who did this not only found the mathematical threshold with relationship to air friction, but she had a ton of fun.

5. The ideal ratio of baking soda to vinegar to make a fire extinguisher.

Another great start. Easy to measure and track, leads to a logical question that can either be supported or refuted with the data.

Each of those topics *measures* one thing such as the amount of sugar, the concentration of soapy water, or the ideal size. If you start with an idea that allows you to measure something, then you can change it, ask questions, explore, and ultimately make a *prediction*, also called a *hypothesis*, and experiment to find out if you are correct. Here are some well-meaning but misguided entries:

Science Reports, <u>not Projects</u>
1. Dinosaurs!

OK, great. Everyone loves dinosaurs but where is the experiment? Did you find a new dinosaur? Is Jurassic Park alive and well, and we are headed there to breed, drug, or in some way test them? Probably not. This was a report on T. rex. Cool, but not a science fair project. And judging by the protest that this kid's mom put up when the kid didn't get his usual "A", it is a safe bet that she put a lot of time in and shared in the disappointment.

More Reports &

2. Our Friend the Sun

Another very large topic, no pun intended. This could be a great topic. Sunlight is fascinating. It can be split, polarized, reflected, refracted, measured, collected, converted. However, this poor kid simply chose to write about the size of the sun, regurgitating facts about its features, cycles, and other astrofacts while simultaneously offending the American Melanoma Survivors Society. Just kidding about that last part.

3. Smokers' Poll

A lot of folks think that they are headed in the right direction here. Again, it depends on how the kid attacks the idea. Are they going to single out race? Heredity? Shoe size? What exactly are they after here? The young lady who did this report chose to make it more of a psychology-studies effort than a scientific report. She wanted to know family income, if they fought with their parents, how much stress was on the job, and so on. All legitimate concerns but not placed in the right slot.

4. The Majestic Moose

If you went out and caught the moose, drugged it to see the side effects for disease control, or even mated it with an elk to determine if you could create an animal that would become the spokesanimal for the Alabama Dairy Farmers' Got Melk? promotion, that would be fine. But, another fact-filled report should be filed with the English teacher.

5. How Tadpoles Change into Frogs

Great start, but they forgot to finish the statement. We know how tadpoles change into frogs. What we don't know is how tadpoles change into frogs if they are in an altered environment, if they are hatched out of cycle, if they are stuck under the tire of an off-road vehicle blatantly driving through a protected wetland area. That's what we want to know. How tadpoles change into frogs, if, when, or under what measurable circumstances.

Now that we have beat the chicken squat out of this introduction, we are going to show you how to pick a topic that can be adapted to become a successful science fair project after one more thought.

One Final Comment

A Gentle Reminder

Quite often I discuss the scientific method with moms and dads, teachers and kids, and get the impression that, according to their understanding, there is one, and only one, scientific method. This is not necessarily true. There are lots of ways to investigate the world we live in and on.

Paleontologists dig up dead animals and plants but have no way to conduct experiments on them. They're dead. Albert Einstein, the most famous scientist of the last century and probably on everybody's starting five of all time, never did experiments. He was a theoretical physicist, which means that he came up with a hypothesis, skipped over collecting materials for things like black holes and space-time continuums, didn't experiment on anything or even collect data. He just went straight from hypothesis to conclusion, and he's still considered part of the scientific community. You'll probably follow the six steps we outline but keep an open mind.

Project Planner

This outline is designed to give you a specific set of time lines to follow as you develop your science fair project. Most teachers will give you 8 to 11 weeks notice for this kind of assignment. We are going to operate from the shorter time line with our suggested schedule, which means that the first thing you need to do is get a calendar.

A. The suggested time to be devoted to each item is listed in parentheses next to that item. Enter the date of the Science Fair and then, using the calendar, work backward entering dates.

B. As you complete each item, enter the date that you completed it in the column between the goal (due date) and project item.

Goal   Completed   Project Item

1. Generate a Hypothesis (2 weeks)

_____   _____   Review Idea Section, pp. 194–197
_____   _____   Try Several Experiments
_____   _____   Hypothesis Generated
_____   _____   Finished Hypothesis Submitted
_____   _____   Hypothesis Approved

2. Gather Background Information (1 week)

_____   _____   Concepts/Discoveries Written Up
_____   _____   Vocabulary/Glossary Completed
_____   _____   Famous Scientists in Field

& Time Line

Goal   *Completed*   *Project Item*

3. Design an Experiment (1 week)

_____ _____ Procedure Written
_____ _____ Lab Safety Review Completed
_____ _____ Procedure Approved
_____ _____ Data Tables Prepared
_____ _____ Materials List Completed
_____ _____ Materials Acquired

4. Perform the Experiment (2 weeks)

_____ _____ Scheduled Lab Time

5. Collect and Record Experimental Data (part of 4)

_____ _____ Data Tables Completed
_____ _____ Graphs Completed
_____ _____ Other Data Collected and Prepared

6. Present Your Findings (2 weeks)

_____ _____ Rough Draft of Paper Completed
_____ _____ Proofreading Completed
_____ _____ Final Report Completed
_____ _____ Display Completed
_____ _____ Oral Report Outlined on Index Cards
_____ _____ Practice Presentation of Oral Report
_____ _____ Oral Report Presentation
_____ _____ Science Fair Setup
_____ _____ Show Time!

Scientific Method
• Step 1 •
The Hypothesis

Opposites Attract • B. K. Hixson

The Hypothesis

A hypothesis is an educated guess. It is a statement of what you think will probably happen. It is also the most important part of your science fair project because it directs the entire process. It determines what you study, the materials you will need, and how the experiment will be designed, carried out, and evaluated. Needless to say, you need to put some thought into this part.

There are four steps to generating a hypothesis:

Step One • Pick a Topic
Preferably something that you are interested in studying. We would like to politely recommend that you take a peek at physical science ideas (physics and chemistry) if you are a rookie and this is one of your first shots at a science fair project. These kinds of lab ideas allow you to repeat experiments quickly. There is a lot of data that can be collected, and there is a huge variety to choose from.

If you are having trouble finding an idea, all you have to do is pick up a compilation of science activities (like this one) and start thumbing through it. Go to the local library or head to a bookstore and you will find a wide and ever-changing selection to choose from. Find a topic that interests you and start reading. At some point an idea will catch your eye, and you will be off to the races.

Pick An Idea You Like

We hope you find an idea you like between the covers of this book. But we also realize that 1) there are more ideas about magnetism than we have included in this book, and 2) other kinds of presentations, or methods of writing labs, may be just what you need to trigger a new idea or put a different spin on things. So, without further adieu, we introduce you to several additional titles that may be of help to you in developing a science fair project.

For Older Kids . . .

1. *The Cool Hot Rod & Other Electrifying Experiments on Energy & Matter. Written by Paul Doherty, Don Rathjen, and the Exploratorium Teacher Institute. ISBN 0-471-11518-5 Published by John Wiley & Sons, Inc. 99 pages.*

This is another fantastic book from our favorite hands-on science center, the Exploratorium in San Francisco, California. It contains twenty-two science "snacks." These are mini-versions of the larger exhibits that you can find at the Exploratorium. Each snack has been designed by classroom teachers and is kid-tested. In addition to sections giving an overview, a list of materials, assembly instructions (with estimated times), things to do and notice, and questions about what is going on, there is also an etc. section that will give you ideas for developing the lab further. The book also comes with excellent illustrations and photographs to guide you in the construction of the lab.

2. *Electricity & Magnetism FUNdamentals. Written by Robert W. Wood. Illustrated by Bill Wright. ISBN 0-7910-4841-1 Published by Chelsea House Publishers. 132 pages.*

This is an excellent resource for both electricity and magnetism. Twenty-eight lab activities are presented in a clear and concise manner. The author has also added fun facts to go with the clear illustrations and extension ideas.

3. *The Usborne Book Batteries and Magnets. Written by Paula Borton and Vicki Cave. Published by Usborne Publishing Ltd. 32 pages.*

This is a very colorful book that contains 15 well-illustrated science projects for kids. Each lab write-up explains how to build the project and also has actual photos of the finished idea. Wonderful applications of magnetism and electricity that give the kids an opportunity to explore some of their artistic tendencies as well.

4. *Magnetism. Written by John Woodruff. ISBN 0-8172-4946-X Published by Raintree Steck Vaughn Publishers, Inc. 48 pages.*

Twenty lab activities are presented in another colorful book that guides the student through the projects using clear, easy-to-follow photographs. Each lab activity is introduced through a paragraph that reviews the concept being explored. The materials are identified and easy-to-follow instructions guide the student to completing the project. Also includes follow-up ideas.

5. *The Science Book of Magnets. Written by Neil Ardley. ISBN 0-15-200581-1 Published by Harcourt, Brace, Jovanovich. 29 pages.*

Fifteen different projects that take basic ideas about magnetism and turn them into fun projects for kids. Each lab activity is photographed each step of the way and is explained in clear and easy-to-follow terms.

6. *Physics for Every Kid. Written by Janice Van Cleave. ISBN 0-471-52505-7 Published by John Wiley & Sons. 192 pages.*

Magnetism is one topic in the field of physics. This book has several lab activities devoted to magnets and magnetism that touch on the basic ideas. Instructions and explanations are abbreviated compared with other books. Good general resource.

Develop an Original Idea

Step Two • Do the Lab

Choose a lab activity that looks interesting and try the experiment. Some kids make the mistake of thinking that all you have to do is find a lab in a book, repeat the lab, and you are on the gravy train with biscuit wheels. Your goal is to ask an ORIGINAL question, not repeat an experiment that has been done a bazillion times before.

As you do the lab, be thinking not only about the data you are collecting, but of ways you could adapt or change the experiment to find out new information. The point of the science fair project is to have you become an actual scientist and contribute a little bit of new knowledge to the world.

You know that they don't pay all of those engineers good money to sit around and repeat other people's lab work. The company wants new ideas so if you are able to generate and explore new ideas you become very valuable, not only to that company but to society. It is the question-askers that find cures for diseases, create new materials, figure out ways to make existing machines energy efficient, and change the way that we live. For the purpose of illustration, we are going to take a lab titled, "Prisms, Water Prisms." from another book, *Photon U*, and run it through the rest of the process. The lab uses a tub of water, an ordinary mirror, and light to create a prism that splits the light into the spectrum of a rainbow. Cool. Easy to do. Not expensive and open to all kinds of adaptations, including the four that we discuss on the next page.

Step Three • *Bend, Fold, Spindle, & Mutilate Your Lab*

Once you have picked out an experiment, ask if it is possible to do any of the following things to modify it into an original experiment. You want to try and change the experiment to make it more interesting and find out one new, small piece of information.

Heat it	Freeze it	Reverse it	Double it
Bend it	Invert it	Poison it	Dehydrate it
Drown it	Stretch it	Fold it	Ignite it
Split it	Irradiate it	Oxidize it	Reduce it
Chill it	Speed it up	Color it	Grease it
Expand it	Substitute it	Remove it	Slow it down

If you take a look at our examples, that's exactly what we did to the main idea. We took the list of 24 different things that you could do to an experiment—not nearly all of them by the way—and tried a couple of them out on the prism setup.

Double it: Get a second prism and see if you can continue to separate the colors farther by lining up a second prism in the rainbow of the first.

Reduce it: Figure out a way to gather up the colors that have been produced and mix them back together to produce white light again.

Reverse it: Experiment with moving the flashlight and paper closer to the mirror and farther away. Draw a picture and be able to predict what happens to the size and clarity of the rainbow image.

Substitute it: You can also create a rainbow on a sunny day using a garden hose with a fine-spray nozzle attached. Set the nozzle adjustment so that a fine mist is produced and move the mist around in the sunshine until you see the rainbow. This works better if the sun is lower in the sky; late afternoon is best.

Hypothesis Work Sheet

Step Three (Expanded) • *Bend, Fold, Spindle Work Sheet*

This work sheet will give you an opportunity to work through the process of creating an original idea.

A. Write down the lab idea that you want to mangle.

_____

_____

_____

_____

B. List the possible variables you could change in the lab.

i. _____

ii. _____

iii. _____

iv. _____

v. _____

CMON.
HE SAID TO
STRETCH IT.

C. Take one variable listed in section B and apply one of the 24 changes listed below to it. Write that change down and state your new lab idea in the space below. Do that with three more changes.

Heat it	Freeze it	Reverse it	Double it
Bend it	Invert it	Poison it	Dehydrate it
Drown it	Stretch it	Fold it	Ignite it
Split it	Irradiate it	Oxidize it	Reduce it
Chill it	Speed it up	Color it	Grease it
Expand it	Substitute it	Remove it	Slow it down

i. _____

_____

_____

_____

ii. _____

_____

_____

_____

iii. _____

_____

_____

_____

iv. _____

_____ STRETCHING!

_____

_____

Step Four • Create an Original Idea— Your Hypothesis
    Your hypothesis should be stated as an opinion. You've done
the basic experiment, you've made observations, you're not stupid.
Put two and two together and make a PREDICTION. Be sure that you
are experimenting with just a single variable.

    A. State your hypothesis in the space below. List the variable.
    i. _____

_____

_____

_____

ii. Variable tested: _____

Sample Hypothesis Work Sheet

On the previous two pages is a work sheet that will help you develop your thoughts and a hypothesis. Here is sample of the finished product to help you understand how to use it.

A. Write down the lab idea that you want to mutilate.

A mirror is placed in a tub of water. A beam of light is focused through the water onto the mirror, producing a rainbow on the wall.

B. List the possible variables you could change in the lab.
  i. **Source of light**
  ii. **The liquid in the tub**
  iii. **The distance from flashlight to mirror**

C. Take one variable listed in section B and apply one of the 24 changes to it. Write that change down and state your new lab idea in the space below.

The shape of the beam of light can be controlled by making and placing cardboard filters over the end of the flashlight. Various shapes such as circles, squares, and slits will produce different quality rainbows.

D. State your hypothesis in the space below. List the variable. Be sure that when you write the hypothesis you are stating an idea and not asking a question.

Hypothesis: The narrower the beam of light the tighter, brighter, and more focused the reflected rainbow will appear.

Variable tested: **The opening on the filter**

Scientific Method
• Step 2 •
Gather Information

Gather Information

Read about your topic and find out what we already know. Check books, videos, the Internet, and movies, talk with experts in the field, and molest an encyclopedia or two. Gather as much information as you can before you begin planning your experiment.

In particular, there are several things that you will want to pay special attention to and that should accompany any good science fair project.

A. Major Scientific Concepts

Be sure that you research and explain the main idea(s) that is / are driving your experiment. It may be a law of physics or chemical rule or an explanation of an aspect of plant physiology.

B. Scientific Words

As you use scientific terms in your paper, you should also define them in the margins of the paper or in a glossary at the end of the report. You cannot assume that everyone knows about geothermal energy transmutation in sulfur-loving bacterium. Be prepared to define some new terms for them. . . and scrub your hands really well when you are done if that is your project.

C. Historical Perspective

When did we first learn about this idea, and who is responsible for getting us this far? You need to give a historical perspective with names, dates, countries, awards, and other recognition.

Building a Research Foundation

1. This sheet is designed to help you organize your thoughts and give you some ideas on where to look for information on your topic. When you prepare your lab report, you will want to include the background information outlined below.

   A. *Major Scientific Concepts (Two is plenty.)*

   i. _____

   _____

   _____

   _____

   ii. _____

   _____

   _____

   _____

   B. *Scientific Words (No more than 10)*

   i. _____

   ii. _____

   iii. _____

   iv. _____

   v. _____

   vi. _____

   vii. _____

   viii. _____

   ix. _____

   x. _____

   C. *Historical Perspective*
      Add this as you find it.

2. There are several sources of information that are available to help you fill in the details from the previous page.

A. *Contemporary Print Resources*
   (Magazines, Newspapers, Journals)

   i. _____

   ii. _____

   iii. _____

   iv. _____

   v. _____

   vi. _____

B. *Other Print Resources*
   (Books, Encyclopedias, Dictionaries, Textbooks)

   i. _____

   ii. _____

   iii. _____

   iv. _____

   v. _____

   vi. _____

C. *Celluloid Resources*
   (Films, Filmstrips, Videos)

   i. _____

   ii. _____

   iii. _____

   iv. _____

   v. _____

   vi. _____

D. *Electronic Resources:*
   (Internet Website Addresses, DVDs, MP3s)

    i. _____

    ii. _____

    iii. _____

    iv. _____

    v. _____

    vi. _____

    vii. _____

    viii. _____

    ix. _____

    x. _____

E. *Human Resources*
   (Scientists, Engineers, Professionals, Professors, Teachers)

    i. _____

    ii. _____

    iii. _____

    iv. _____

    v. _____

    vi. _____

You may want to keep a record of all of your research and add it to the back of the report as an Appendix. Some teachers who are into volume think this is really cool. Others, like myself, find it a pain in the tuchus. No matter what you do, be sure to keep an accurate record of where you find data. If you quote from a report word for word, be sure to give proper credit with either a footnote or parenthetical reference, this is very important for credibility and accuracy. This is will keep you out of trouble with plagiarism (copying without giving credit).

Scientific Method
· Step 3 ·
Design Your Experiment

Acquire Your Lab Materials

The purpose of this section is to help you plan your experiment. You'll make a map of where you are going, how you want to get there, and what you will take along.

List the materials you will need to complete your experiment in the table below. Be sure to list multiples if you will need more than one item. Many science materials double as household items in their spare time. Check around the house before you buy anything from a science supply company or hardware store. For your convenience, we have listed some suppliers on page 19 of this book.

Material	Qty.	Source	$
1.			
2.			
3.			
4.			
5.			
6.			
7.			
8.			
9.			
10.			
11.			
12.			

Total $_____

Outline Your Experiment

This sheet is designed to help you outline your experiment. If you need more space, make a copy of this page to finish your outline. When you are done with this sheet, review it with an adult, make any necessary changes, review safety concerns on the next page, prepare your data tables, gather your equipment, and start to experiment.

In the space below, list what you are going to do in the order you are going to do it.

i. _____

_____

_____

_____

ii. _____

_____

_____

_____

iii. _____

_____

_____

_____

iv. _____

_____

_____

_____

v. _____

_____

_____

_____

Evaluate Safety Concerns

We have included an overall safety section in the front of this book on pages 16–18, but there are some very specific questions you need to ask, and prepare for, depending on the needs of your experiment. If you find that you need to prepare for any of these safety concerns, place a check mark next to the letter.

_____ *A. Goggles & Eyewash Station*
If you are mixing chemicals or working with materials that might splinter or produce flying objects, goggles and an eyewash station or sink with running water should be available.

_____ *B. Ventilation*
If you are mixing chemicals that could produce fire, smoke, fumes, or obnoxious odors, you will need to use a vented hood or go outside and perform the experiment in the fresh air.

_____ *C. Fire Blanket or Fire Extinguisher*
If you are working with potentially combustible chemicals or electricity, a fire blanket and extinguisher nearby are a must.

_____ *D. Chemical Disposal*
If your experiment produces a poisonous chemical or there are chemical-filled tissues (as in dissected animals), you may need to make arrangements to dispose of the by-products from your lab.

_____ *E. Electricity*
If you are working with materials and developing an idea that uses electricity, make sure that the wires are in good repair, that the electrical demand does not exceed the capacity of the supply, and that your work area is grounded.

_____ *F. Emergency Phone Numbers*
Look up and record the following phone numbers for the Fire Department: _____ , Poison Control: _____ , and Hospital: _____. Post them in an easy-to-find location.

Prepare Data Tables

Finally, you will want to prepare your data tables and have them ready to go before you start your experiment. Each data table should be easy to understand and easy for you to use.

A good data table has a **title** that describes the information being collected, and it identifies the **variable** and the **unit** being collected on each data line. The variable is *what* you are measuring and the unit is *how* you are measuring it. They are usually written like this:

Variable (unit), or to give you some examples:

Time (seconds)
Distance (meters)
Electricity (volts)

An example of a well-prepared data table looks like the sample below. We've cut the data table into thirds because the book is too small to display the whole line.

Determining the Boiling Point of Compound X$_1$

Time (min.)	0	1	2	3	4	5	6
Temp. (°C)							

Time (min.)	7	8	9	10	11	12	13
Temp. (°C)							

Time (min.)	14	15	16	17	18	19	20
Temp. (°C)							

Scientific Method
• Step 4 •
Conduct the Experiment

Lab Time

It's time to get going. You've generated a hypothesis, collected the materials, written out the procedure, checked the safety issues, and prepared your data tables. Fire it up. Here's the short list of things to remember as you experiment.

_____ *A. Follow the Procedure, Record Any Changes*

Follow your own directions specifically as you wrote them. If you find the need to change the procedure once you are into the experiment, that's fine; it's part of the process. Make sure to keep detailed records of the changes. When you repeat the experiment a second or third time, follow the new directions exactly.

_____ *B. Observe Safety Rules*

It's easier to complete the lab activity if you are in the lab rather than the emergency room.

_____ *C. Record Data Immediately*

Collect temperatures, distances, voltages, revolutions, and any other variables and immediately record them into your data table. Do not think you will be able to remember them and fill everything in after the lab is completed.

_____ *D. Repeat the Experiment Several Times*

The more data that you collect, the better. It will give you a larger data base and your averages are more meaningful. As you do multiple experiments, be sure to identify each data set by date and time so you can separate them out.

_____ *E. Prepare for Extended Experiments*

Some experiments require days or weeks to complete, particularly those with plants and animals or the growing of crystals. Prepare a safe place for your materials so your experiment can continue undisturbed while you collect the data. Be sure you've allowed enough time for your due date.

Scientific Method
• Step 5 •
Collect and Display Data

Types of Graphs

This section will give you some ideas on how you can display the information you are going to collect as a graph. A graph is simply a picture of the data that you gathered portrayed in a manner that is quick and easy to reference. There are four kinds of graphs described on the next two pages. If you find you need a leg up in the graphing department, we have a book in the series called *Data Tables & Graphing*. It will guide you through the process.

Line and Bar Graphs

These are the most common kinds of graphs. The most consistent variable is plotted on the "x", or horizontal, axis and the more temperamental variable is plotted along the "y", or vertical, axis. Each data point on a line graph is recorded as a dot on the graph and then all of the dots are connected to form a picture of the data. A bar graph starts on the horizontal axis and moves up to the data line.

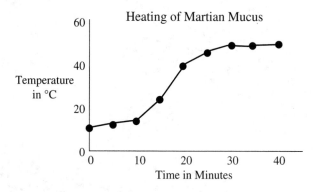

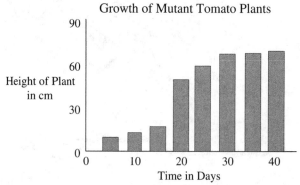

Best Fit Graphs

A best fit graph was created to show averages or trends rather than specific data points. The data that has been collected is plotted on a graph just as on a line graph, but instead of drawing a line from point to point to point, which sometimes is impossible anyway, you just free hand a line that hits "most of the data."

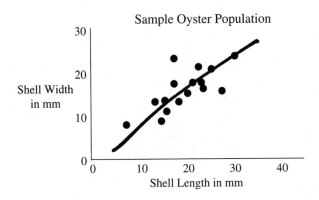

Pie Graphs

Pie graphs are used to show relationships between different groups. All of the data is totaled up and a percentage is determined for each group. The pie is then divided to show the relationship of one group to another.

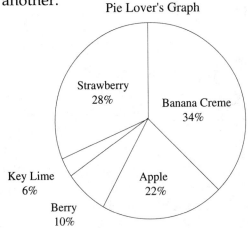

Other Kinds of Data

1. Written Notes & Observations

This is the age-old technique used by all scientists. Record your observations in a lab book. Written notes can be made quickly as the experiment is proceeding, and they can then be expounded upon later. Quite often notes made in the heat of an experiment are revisited during the evaluation portion of the process, and they can shed valuable light on how or why the experiment went the way it did.

2. Drawings

Quick sketches as well as fully developed drawings can be used as a way to report data for a science experiment. Be sure to title each drawing and, if possible, label what it is that you are looking at. Drawings that are actual size are best.

3. Photographs, Videotapes, and Audiotapes

Usually better than drawings, quicker, and more accurate, but you do have the added expense and time of developing the film. However, they can often capture images and details that are not usually seen by the naked eye.

4. The Experiment Itself

Some of the best data you can collect and present is the actual experiment itself. Nothing will speak more effectively for you than the plants you grew, the specimens you collected, or that big pile of tissue that was an armadillo you peeled from the tread of an 18-wheeler.

Scientific Method
• Step 6 •
Present Your Ideas

Oral Report Checklist

It is entirely possible that you will be asked to make an oral presentation to your classmates. This will give you an opportunity to explain what you did and how you did it. Quite often this presentation is part of your overall score, so if you do well, it will enhance your chances for one of the bigger awards.

To prepare for your oral report, your science fair presentation should include the following components:

Physical Display

_____a.   freestanding display board
                    hypothesis
                    data tables, graphs, photos, etc.
                    abstract (short summary)

_____b.   actual lab setup (equipment)

Oral Report

_____a.   hypothesis or question
_____b.   background information
                    concepts
                    word definitions
                    history or scientists
_____c.   experimental procedure
_____d.   data collected
                    data tables
                    graphs
                    photos or drawings
_____e.   conclusions and findings
_____f.   ask for questions

Set the display board up next to you on the table. Transfer the essential information to index cards. Use the index cards for reference, but do not read from them. Speak in a clear voice, hold your head up, and make eye contact with your peers. Ask if there are any questions before you finish and sit down.

Written Report Checklist

Next up is the written report, also called your lab write-up. After you compile or sort the data you have collected during the experiment and evaluate the results, you will be able to come to a conclusion about your hypothesis. Remember, disproving an idea is as valuable as proving it.

This sheet is designed to help you write up your science fair project and present your data in an organized manner. This is a final checklist for you.

To prepare your write-up, your science fair report should include the following components:

_____	a.	binder
_____	b.	cover page, title, & your name
_____	c.	abstract (one paragraph summary)
_____	d.	table of contents with page numbers
_____	e.	hypothesis or question
_____	f.	background information
		concepts
		word definitions
		history or scientists
_____	g.	list of materials used
_____	h.	experimental procedure
		written description
		photo or drawing of setup
_____	i.	data collected
		data tables
		graphs
		photos or drawings
_____	j.	conclusions and findings
_____	k.	glossary of terms
_____	l.	references

Display Checklist

2. Prepare your display to accompany the report. A good display should include the following:

Freestanding Display

_____ a.   freestanding cardboard back
_____ b.   title of experiment
_____ c.   your name
_____ d.   hypothesis
_____ e.   findings of the experiment
_____ f.   photo or illustrations of equipment
_____ g.   data tables or graphs

Additional Display Items

_____ h.   a copy of the write-up
_____ i.   actual lab equipment setup

Glossary,
Index,
and
More Ideas

Glossary

Alligator leads

Also known as test leads. These wires have clamps that resemble the head of an alligator on both ends. The clamps make it easy to attach the wire to a variety of different objects and hold it in place. They are used for decorative purposes in other circles.

Armature

The part of a motor that spins. It consists of a coil of wire that experiences a rapid change in direction of its magnetic field. This change, in the presence of a standing magnetic field, causes the armature to spin.

Bipolar Molecules

Molecules that have a positive end and a negative end, which in essence creates a mini-magnet. Water is an excellent example of a common bipolar molecule.

Charge, electrostatic

An accumulation or collection of a large number of electrons that are not stored in a chemical battery. When you walk across a carpet in wool socks and then touch a doorknob, that is an electrostatic charge.

Compass

A instrument that consists of a magnetized needle suspended so that it can rotate freely. The needle responds to the magnetic field of the Earth, indicating magnetic north, or to a stronger more localized magnetic field like a magnet.

Curie Point

The temperature at which a metal can no longer maintain a magnetic field. This happens as the metal is heated and the atoms in the metal start to move around. When they get to the point where they are bouncing around so much that they lose their ability to organize (and maintain a magnetic field), that is called the Curie point.

Demagnetizing
The process of disorienting the atoms in a magnetic substance to the point where they can no longer produce a magnetic field. This can be accomplished by hitting or dropping a magnet or by heating a magnet.

Eddy Currents
Eddy currents are produced when a magnet is dropped through an iron tube. The magnet moving through the tube induces a magnetic field in the tube that in turn interacts with the magnet slowing its descent.

Electromagnet
A magnet that is produced when an iron object is wrapped with conductive wire and then an electric current is applied to the wire. The wire produces a magnetic field that then organizes the iron atoms in the core to produce an even stronger magnet.

Ferrofluid
Sounds like a new drink for bodybuilders, but it is really a colloid composed of incredibly small iron particles suspended in a liquid. When these particles come in contact with a magnetic field, they produce a three-dimensional image of the magnetic field proportional to the strength of the magnetic field.

Galvanometer
An instrument that detects very small amounts of current in a coil of wire. When electricity flows through a wire, a magnetic field immediately surrounds that wire. If a galvanometer is near the wire, it will detect and respond to the magnetic field.

Iron Filings
Whiskers shaved off a magnet. Just kidding—actually very small magnetized iron particles that respond to magnetic fields. They can be used to detect magnetic fields, to play games, or as filler in cereal.

Glossary

Lodestone
A naturally occurring magnet. Usually associated with iron deposits. This mineral, also called magnetite, was used to make the original compasses.

Magnet
A material composed of either iron, nickel, or sometimes neodium, that contains an internal pattern of well-organized atoms that work together to produce a magnetic field and produce magnetic effects.

Magnet, bar
Social place where magnets go after work. Just kidding. A pair of long skinny metal magnets that have distinct poles. When they are stored in their container, they should be north to south and south to north.

Magnet, book
A ceramic magnet that is produced and magnetized as a long block and then sliced like a loaf of bread. This produces the poles on the flat surfaces of the magnet unlike the bar magnets.

Magnet, cow
So named for the animal they are supposed to help. Cows, being the brilliant animals that they are, eat all kinds of things including barbed wire, tin cans, and old hubcaps—certainly not lacking in iron but not so good for the multiple stomachs. So, farmers insert very powerful magnets into the first stomach of the cow to keep the metal from passing all the way through the cow and causing significant damage or death.

Magnet, donut
So named for its shape—a round magnet with a hole in it. Magnetism does not improve if the magnet is dunked in coffee.

Magnet, horseshoe
A bar magnet bent so that it is shaped like a horseshoe.

Magnet, levitating
When two magnets are placed like pole to like pole, north to north or south to south, the poles repel one another, or push one another away. If the magnets are held in a stable position, they are said to be levitating.

Magnet, wand
A magnet that has been imbedded in a plastic or wooden handle so that it can be manipulated easily.

Magnetic Attraction
The movement of two oppositely charged objects toward one another. Typically the north and south poles of a magnet. It could also be the positive and negative ends of a bipolar molecule.

Magnetic Field
The invisible influence surrounding a magnetized object that attracts or repels (drives apart) other magnetic materials. The size and strength of the magnetic field is directly correlated to how the particles in the material are organized.

Magnetic Field of Earth
An invisible magnetic field that surrounds the Earth beginning at the North Pole and extending to the South Pole. This magnetic field influences the movement of charged particles produced by the Sun and other stars as they enter the Earth's atmosphere.

Magnetic Mapping
The process of using either a compass, iron filings, or Ferrofluid to detect and locate the presence of magnetic fields around objects. The map describes the size of the field and the direction that it is moving at any particular point in space.

Glossary

Magnetic Wire, electrified
Any wire that conducts electricity is also surrounded by a magnetic field. If the direction of the movement of the electrons changes, the magnetic field also changes direction. If the electricity is removed, the magnetic field ceases to exist.

Magnetic Induction
The movement of electrons in a wire can also be accomplished by inducing them to move by using a magnet. This is most commonly accomplished using a coil of wire. When a magnet is inserted in the coil of wire, an electric current starts to flow and a magnetic field is produced— simply another wonder of nature.

Magnetic Repulsion
The opposite of magnetic attraction and not unlike eating something that you do not really like—you want to push it away from you as fast as possible. In the case of magnets, like poles repel.

Magnetic Shielding
A material, like iron, that prohibits the passage of the magnetic field through it. Most things like wood, plastic, cloth, glass, or even tissue, do not seem to mind allowing magnetic fields to pass through them. Others, like iron, do. They redirect the magnetic field internally without letting it get all the way through. Congress has used this model for years when dealing with issues like campaign contribution reform and funding for tobacco companies.

Meniscus
A dip in a pool of water—not to be confused with taking a dip in a pool of water. This one is caused by the cohesion of water molecules with the sides of the container.

Motor

A coil of wire that spins in the presence of a permanent magnet. Motors can do all kinds of work and are used in blenders, cars, mixers, washing machines, rock crushers, and just about every other widget that we buy these days.

Motor Effect

The movement of a loop of wire in the presence of a magnetic field. This movement provides the initial push to get the motor turning.

Nonpermeable Materials

Materials that do not allow magnetic fields to pass through them. They instead choose to reroute the magnetic field internally, sending it back to its maker without allowing it out their other side.

Permeable Materials

Materials that do not allow magnetic fields to pass through them, which is a very large and popular club. Most materials allow for magnetic fields to pass through them easily and quickly. Iron and a host of other metals have other opinions.

Poles, magnet

All magnets, regardless of size, have a two opposite poles, north and south. These poles are the strongest part of the magnet and are the parts that interact with other magnetic materials.

Right-Hand Rule

This is a simple rule that allows you to determine the direction of a magnetic field around a wire if you know which way the current is flowing through a wire. Using your right hand, simply stick your thumb up in the direction the current is flowing and your fingers, held in a C position, will indicate the direction of the magnetic field.

Three-Dimensional Magnetic Mapping

The process of looking at the entire magnetic field surrounding an object—using all three dimensions as opposed to simply using two.

Index

Index

Magnet
Magnetic
Magnets
Meniscus
Motor

More Science Books

Catch a Wave

50 hands-on lab activities that sound off on the topic of noise, vibration, waves, the Doppler Effect and associated ideas.

Thermodynamic Thrills

50 hands-on lab activities that investigate heat via conduction, convection, radiation, specific heat, and temperature.

Relatively Albert

50 hands-on lab activities that explore the world of mechanics, forces, gravity, and Newton's three laws of motion.

Photon U

50 hands-on lab activities from the world of light. Starts with the basic colors of the rainbow and works you way up to polarizing filters and UV light.

Electron Herding 101

50 hands-on lab activities that introduce static electricity, circuit electricity, and include a number of fun, and very easy-to-build projects.

Junior Chemhead

50 hands-on lab activities that delve into the world of chemistry and the characteristics of atoms, molecules, and other basic chemistry ideas for young chemists.